TRAINING A
YOUNG POINTER

TRAINING A YOUNG POINTER

*How the Experts Developed
My Bird Dog and Me*

JOE HEALY

STACKPOLE
BOOKS

Published by
STACKPOLE BOOKS
5067 Ritter Road
Mechanicsburg, PA 17055
www.stackpolebooks.com

Printed in the U.S.A.

First edition

10 9 8 7 6 5 4 3 2 1

Photographs by the author except where noted.

Library of Congress Cataloging-in-Publication Data
Healy, Joseph, 1967–
  Training a young pointer: how the experts developed my bird dog and me / Joseph Healy.
    p. cm.
  Includes bibliographical references and index.
  ISBN 0-8117-0143-3 (hardcover)
  1. Pointing dogs—Training. I. Title.

SF428.5.H36 2005
636.752'5—dc22

2004030248

ISBN 978-0-8117-0143-3

In memory of
John Offerman and Tim Leary

"There is nothing mystical about developing a dog: it is basically patience, good judgment, tenacity, kindness, understanding, consistency, and a lot of hard but pleasant work. As Thomas Edison said—5 percent inspiration and 95 percent perspiration."

—*Robert G. Wehle,* Snakefoot

CONTENTS

Introduction

I HURRIED OVER SNAGS AND KICKED THROUGH PRICKERS TO KEEP PACE
with the lithe white dog as she plunged into the tag alders, her nose
high and at full-alert status, her torso low as she cut sharply around
sapling-size trees like a slalom skier attacking gates, her whippy tail
beating as a metronome. "She's birdy, watch her," her owner yelled to
me. No sooner had he said that than the dog came to a full stop,
twisting her head and shoulders around herself, bowing low with
haunches high, tail now a spike. The beeper collar she wore for locat-
ing purposes began to bleat in measured tones every second, as it was
programmed to do when the dog wearing it stopped moving.
Brendan shouted, "She's on point! You see her?"

I ducked under and bulled through the tight clutch of latticed
leafless tree limbs, heading toward a small creek, all the while keeping
a close watch on her rigid white body. Her spiky tail was rigid and
trembling. Her shoulders shook too, and her haunches shivered. But
her head was rock solid. I whispered, "Whoa"—feeling slightly guilty
about it, I must admit; she wasn't my dog to command, but her owner
was yards behind us, and not having a dog of my own, I got a slight

thrill from thinking I was in charge. Brendan told me to go in and flush the bird; the covert meant it was a tight-holding woodcock, a species that prefers wet-bottomed areas such as alder stands. I readied to shoulder my gun as I stepped forward.

I walked two steps past Nell and kicked with my right boot at the brush of matted goldenrod stalks and brown grass, sweeping back and forth with my toe. I saw the bird before it flushed—a compacted bundle of feathers in earth-tone browns shading to beige and rust-orange nestled at the base of an alder pole. It seemed to fluff its breast as I leaned onto the balls of my feet to ready for the shot. The bird burst into motion, a sort of feathered jack-in-the-box, elevating in an instant in a helicoptering woodcock flush. As it leveled off above the twelve-foot alder tops, I flicked off the shotgun's safety and shot once. Nell, the pointer, looked up at me and then crept forward to point another bird. I shot that one too. I swear I saw Nell smile as she retrieved the first bird when Brendan, her owner, commanded her, "Fetch." Carrying that bird back to Brendan, Nell had feathers pasted to the sides of her mouth, decorating her white snout and pinkish nose. We were hunting about a mile from my house in southern Vermont. The birds, two woodcock, were warm and heavy in the game pouch in the back of my hunting vest as we made the short walk back to my truck.

I had hunted over Nell, my friend Brendan Banahan's English pointer, a few other times through the years. She was the most athletic dog I'd ever seen work in the woods, neither methodical and close-ranging like an English setter nor nose-to-the-ground, forest-vacuuming like some Brittanys. Nell was an athlete, a sprinter. Nell broad-jumped the creek, she didn't wallow through it. Nell vaulted the deadfall, she didn't belly-crawl under. Nell was ten or eleven when I shot that brace of woodcock over her, a seasoned and mature pointer. She died in 2002 at fifteen, sadly, though she lived a long life for a pointer. I shot two woodcock over her in the autumn of 2001, too, her last season. They were the last birds she pointed. She was a wondrous dog, and I miss her, though never more than Brendan does. Nell was seasoned, and though still prone to being a "blockhead," as Brendan called her, she was gorgeous and majestic when on point. If I had a dog, I said, it would be an English pointer.

In 1999, I made good on that promise.

From the day I brought Reilly home when she was ten weeks old, I had no idea how to start grooming her to be a hunting companion. Within three days, I had read the better part of three dog-training books. None addressed how to train an English pointer her age. I didn't want to know about pitching a pigeon wing or lawn training yet; I wanted to know whether to tell her to come or fetch or, as she ran, say come 'round or quarter or whoa or heel or stop or "Git over here, yuh shit-bird," as I once heard an owner say to his dog before fingering the button on the transmitter he held to send an electrical zap to the nodes of the electronic collar fitted on his dog. And what about training collars? No one I knew had a definite opinion on whether or when to begin using these particular tools. My bird-hunting friends said, "You gotta be careful not to change their personality," mixed with "But you don't wanna spoil the dog." Where to begin?

In my experience, English pointers are best known nowadays as southern or western dogs, hard-working quail runners that bust lespedeza tracts in ninety-degree heat till they're whistled back to the dog wagon and the handler on the quail plantation releases the next wave of dogs to range out in front of the horse-saddled hunters, or as big runners in big-country swales in Montana and the Dakotas where pheasants and prairie birds are found.

In the Northeast, we have other expected pointing-dog breeds, namely English setters, German shorthairs, and Brittany spaniels. These breeds are hardworking and generally close-hunting, which has gained them favor among grouse and woodcock hunters. Still, having hunted over Nell and seeing what she could do, I fell for the sheer athleticism of an English pointer.

In recent years, perhaps because of their popularity as field-trial dogs that are expected to run big and range far, and with the exception most notably of the Elhew pointer bloodline, English pointers have fallen out of favor with Northeastern hunters. (Brendan is the only other hunter I know who has owned and hunted an English pointer.) And in the area of southern Vermont where I lived when I got my first dog, there were no English pointer support groups. But this Yankee boy got himself a pointer.

As a journalist and writer, intensely curious by nature, I wanted to know the right way to go about training this spirited breed. I couldn't find much word-of-mouth support, so I read as much as I could, and then I hired the experts, two pros, to train my dog and, more important, to train me in the process—the latter no doubt a much more challenging and daunting task than the dog work.

Mind you, I'm not lazy; I didn't hire trainers and pay their fees, which so far come to more than $2,500, because I had no time for or interest in the training myself. In fact, I quit my job (partially, at least) in publishing for a year for the express purpose of training my dog and, eventually, to see her trained. But maybe like you, I had no idea where to begin with the training and then where to take the training, in what stages. I feared ruining my dog of her inborn instincts, stepping on her natural abilities, as a result of my own inexperience with the process. So I shelled out the bucks to learn from guys who've trained, cumulatively, thousands of working dogs. And I learned more than I ever expected.

Is taking your dog to a trainer always a satisfying experience? Depends on you, the dog, and the trainer. I was lucky in that I found two trainers who were compassionate to my dog and with whom I became friends as well. I hold the work of these men in such high regard that the guidance they've given my dog would be secondary—

were it not for the fact that her performance is a testament to the work they do, to the training skills they possess. An encomium? Damn right.

I have hunting friends who believe it's foolish to hire a trainer. Such ridicule, too often, stems from the perception that professional hunting-dog trainers are for the rich guy who wants a field-trial-ready animal without getting his hands soiled or blistered or, with ill-tempered dogs, bitten. In my experience, that convention is simply not the case. "There is no short cut to dog training. The best trainer in the world will have to put in just as much time and work on the dog as you would," wrote Robert G. Wehle in his book, *Wing & Shot*. Most owners who take their dogs to trainers do so to have the best possible experience with their dogs in the two-, four-, or, at best, six-week bird-hunting season we have in the field each year. They're not off the hook once the dogs leave the trainers; the work continues. My feeling was, Why not start the work off right?

My friend Larry Kenney, the advertising director of *American Angler* magazine and a longtime owner of versatile dogs who had his youngest dogs—albeit flushing dogs—professionally trained, shared these universal comments on dog training with me:

"As a dyed-in-the-wool flushing-dog guy, I trained my first three dogs, such as that was, all by myself, a springer, a Lab, and then another springer, all females, and all from simple 'both parents hunt' stock. I was pretty satisfied with how they performed for me on a northern Californian's typical list of pheasants, ducks, quail, and the occasional chukar, which is to say they found and put up birds and mostly brought them back when I shot them. But by the time I was into that third dog, the best of the lot, I'd seen how much better fully trained flushing dogs could be, and I determined to set higher goals.

"That was easier said than done given a more-than-full-time job, a family, and a reluctance to really put the screws to a dog when it messed up. To make things tougher, that fourth dog, a big, goony, male springer out of impressive field-trial lines, also met me at every turn with a willful resistance that had me more than once on the verge of *canicide*. I simply wasn't capable enough, or willing enough, to exert the kind of physical force and discipline he needed. So instead of giving up or giving him away, at seven months of age I placed him with a trainer. He stayed for six months, cost me five times what the dog did, and it was some of the best money I ever spent. The pup got intelligent, disciplined training and saw more birds than my other dogs did in a couple of years of hunting. I worked with the dog and the trainer once a week for an hour or so, and not only ended up with a well-started dog who was pretty much steady to wing and shot, but I learned a bunch in the bargain. When I added another dog to the household eight years later, we'd moved to Oregon, but I placed her with another trainer for three months just to start her right on birds, then worked her myself. Again, money more than well spent."

Testify, Larry, testify!

Trainers and happy hunting-dog owners with whom I've spoken always stress that you've got to have realistic expectations for training results. Dropping off a dog at a trainer's kennel and expecting the dog to be field-trial stock or a champion in the woods three months later is usually a recipe for disappointment. The results come over time, depending on the bloodlines and genes of your dog and its ability to be trained. The two trainers who worked with my pointer agreed that some dogs just can't be trained to be top-drawer or even good pointing dogs—they don't have the instinctual stuff to draw out with training. Other dogs may need years of training. Your dog may need only a couple seasons or, in the rare case, just one. But time and repetition trump all, and a professional trainer makes it his job to use both with your dog—and often, with you as well. Bring daily exposure to birds into the mix, and the argument for professional training is hard to refute. Unless, that is, you can provide all the elements of professional training yourself: open spaces for training, lots of pigeons or penned quail, several hours each day for obedience and field-training exercises, and plenty of patience.

I admit that I have little experience and scant authority on matters of bird-dog training, except relating to my first pointing dog, Reilly, and what I've read and sponged up from writers and trainers of great authority. My reason for writing this book, I suppose, is to help others gain confidence in the training of any pointing breed, whether they do the training themselves or hire professional trainers as I did. I know from experience that we can worry more than we need to about the development of dogs; however, we do face the reality of limiting their instinctual growth by overburdening them too quickly or unrealistically with our own expectations. I felt overwhelmed by not having a source that would tell me, "Don't worry, you're doing okay; get help if you need it."

No, I'm not a dog trainer. But I offer in this book much of what I learned in my early years of owning a pointing dog—and what I've learned working with some memorable and talented dog owners and trainers. And when I say "dog" or "hunting dog" throughout this book, I mean the pointing breeds, unless I mention another specific breed. Recollections from my notes and journal entries of the timeline during my dog's first three years, supported by photos, follow in these pages. I hope that sharing what I've learned helps you with the training of your own pointing dog.

Joe Healy
August 2004
East Burke, Vermont

CHAPTER 1

Pointers on Pointers

IF YOU ARE OR INTEND TO BE A FIRST-TIME POINTING-DOG OWNER, YOU either have already chosen a breed with which to work or are contemplating the various choices of pointers available today. English pointer, English setter, Brittany spaniel, vizsla, German shorthaired pointer, weimaraner—these are the workhorses of the pointing-dog world. Which breed you select, and the training you elect to put the dog through, should depend first on what type of hunting you plan to do. Hunting the nation's western prairies requires a big-running dog trained to hunt differently than a northern dog that needs to be attuned to tight woodcock and grouse coverts. The much-respected and widely reputed English pointer breeder and trainer Robert G. Wehle offers superb suggestions along these lines in his book *Wing & Shot;* Kenneth C. Roebuck also offers excellent opinions in *Gun-Dog Training Pointing Dogs.* The best advice I can offer is to know all you can about the breeds with which you may be compatible by thinking hard about your own personality and selecting the breed that complements you.

If, for example, you are high-strung and impatient, don't get an English pointer, which is a generally high-strung and impatient breed and may feed off your type-A personality with negative, overramped results. But if you're athletic and like a brisk pace to your hunting, an English pointer may be heaven-sent. If, however, you view hunting as a leisurely walk in the woods, a hard-charging English pointer or German shorthair will upset your pace; maybe an English setter is better for you.

As Roebuck writes, "It is most essential that you take working ability into consideration first and foremost." You might like the appearance of a certain breed, but it's best to search for a dog that works in a way you can appreciate without getting knotted up with frustration. So think about your personality, and choose a dog you're reasonably certain you can handle. Minimize frustration and you'll be able to properly discipline your dog, without emotion, as you reinforce that which the dog has been trained to do.

Only you can decide what dog is best for you. But I can speak from experience here: When you find the right breed and the right dog, you will be smitten for life. And finding out whether you have the right dog meets the test when you begin training it. That's the path this book follows.

My English pointer, Reilly, just passing her fourth birthday (in human years) as I write this, is not much like me. I'm laid-back, contemplative, and, in my thoughts, obsessive. She's impulsive, quick to act, impatient. We're both athletic and fit—I played soccer in college and still consider myself reasonably fit; she's naturally agile and fit—though she's more of a sprinter whereas I'm quick but slow-footed. Still, I've never questioned whether we fit together. We do. As of this writing, she and I have lasted longer together than any woman and I have. (Although that may have changed by the time you read this book!)

Reilly came to me by some source of fate. This statement does play to my life view—that we all are bystanders, to some degree, to that which fate serves up. My personal code of living is shaped largely by a lifetime of Irish Catholic guilt and repentance and a personal Hindu reprieve gained mostly by studying and assimilating into my life view the hymns of the Upanishads and Tagore, the great Bengali poet, as well as sentiments from the works of the Romantic poets, particularly Wordsworth and Blake. I believe in forces of fate and nature. It's my belief in fate that leads me to acknowledge that this dog and I were meant to teach each other in the ten to fifteen years or so that we'll be together.

It's a clammy tale. Boy wants dog. Live-in girlfriend says no. Months pass. Boy works on girl—on her attitudes, Californian that she is, about hunting. Talks to her about Steinbeck hunting quail—though the truth is he hated to shoot them, he found them so pretty. October leads to November; it's bird-hunting season in Vermont. Boy laments about not having his own dog, and then introduces girl to Nell, his friend and colleague Brendan's pointer. Girl seems to soften her canine opinions. Boy sez, "Honey, I grew up with a hunting dog"—Boy is coy; he had a golden who never took to the field—"and, Girl, you see how good pointers are." Girl sez she loves Boy and will do what she can to make him happy. They are happy. They are a family.

In late November 1999, at Boy's childhood house, Girl and Boy are visiting with Boy's parents, having Thanksgiving dinner and an early birthday celebration for Boy. They talk about Girl and Boy getting a dog. All agree that a dog is a nice first step to what might come after. Wine is poured; toasts are made. Dog means family.

"Granddog," Boy sez to his parents, and they shake their heads and say, "Don't you dare say that till the grandchildren are covered." More wine, more fun. And then a dim Sunday morning. Till Boy opens the *Syracuse Herald American,* November 28 edition, flips to the classified ads, and goes to the "Pets" listing. He scans down to "E" for English pointer. That's past "A" for African grey parrot and Australian cattle dog and "D" for Doberman and dachshund and Dalmatian. Boy sees a listing. He reads it four times to himself before he calls to Girl, who's in the kitchen with his mother, "Girl, I found it!"

The ad reads: "English Pointer Puppies: 'Bird Dog,' registered. Includes shots, wormings & tatoo [*sic*]. Sire is 5x champion, 3x R–U champion, 1999 NYS Dog Of The Year, Comanche's Tonto." It lists a phone number in New York area code 607. Boy has been reading *Shooting Sportsman* and *Gray's Sporting Journal* and *Gun Dog* and *Pointing Dog Journal,* studying the ads in the back of those periodicals, looking for breeders of pointing dogs. He's even thought of running a want ad in one of the fly-fishing magazines for which he works, knowing that fly fishing and bird hunting are closely allied. Now, here in central New York, randomly, in the *Herald American,* his original hometown newspaper, he finds a breeder not far away in southern-central New York.

Boy calls. He leaves a message. He's disappointed because he and Girl could leave his parents' house right now and go have a look at the dogs and the breeder. They are also, right then, he thinks, only about two hours or less from the Elhew compound, owned by Robert Wehle of the Wehle family who in 1932 founded Genesee Brewing Company, and who breeds and raises and trains the best, some think, and probably most expensive pointers in the country. They have an estate, the Wehles, up on Lake Ontario. From Oneida Lake, on which Boy grew up, it is a short drive. But Boy says no, he doesn't want an Elhew/Wehle; frankly, he's intimidated by the notion of having that caliber of dog. He's read that Mr. Wehle interviews all prospective buyers, and Boy's not sure he has the knowledge to pass muster as a champion-dog owner. He wants a beer and a day to think about the dog.

He asks Girl if she'd like a beer. She says yes. He gets them two Labatt Blues. They are a family. Life seems hopeful. . .

My girlfriend, C, raised in heavy-suburban northern California, had no experience with or direct exposure to hunting. Her father didn't hunt; no member of her family did. She didn't oppose or abominate hunting—she had no frame of reference by which to form a strong, determined opinion about it. She had a vague awareness that it was something rural guys simply *did,* though she intimated more than once that it seemed an anachronism in modern culture. However, she wasn't neutral about the prospect of killing a bird or an animal, and she lamented to me that she wished I didn't have to shoot the birds. Bird-hunting friends of mine have similar kinks in their close relationships. "If only there was a way to catch and release birds," Roz Leone, my friend Lee's wife, said to me once. Roz has helped Lee train about a dozen pointing dogs and cares for their three hunting dogs when Lee's away from home. She launches the traps for Lee during shooting practice; she cooks and eats the birds he shoots. Still . . . you can't ignore empathy.

C's grandparents had owned a ranch in California, and visits there took her out of the suburbs and close to the land and to horses and other animals, which gave her fond memories of being outdoors. This rural heritage helped bring her to condone my interest in hunting, yet her permissiveness was tainted by a distain for firearms: She wasn't thrilled that guns were in our house.

But C could see the sport in working with the dog. From the day we brought a pointing dog home, she understood that the dog was bred to be a hunter—that it was born of hunting stock.

I was of that stock, too, I told C.

Ever the facilitator (she was studying for her master's in social work at the time), C didn't object to my plans to train a working dog. Indeed, she never vetoed the plan to have the dog at a kennel, full-time, for more than three months during the summer of 2000, before the dog had even turned a year old. I'd like to think that C admired, or at least respected, my conviction to have the dog trained in the most complete way I could. She just didn't want to think too deeply about the denouement of the act of hunting; she didn't want to see the guns uncased. I didn't force the issue. We had a workable détente.

Ultimately, I figured C's tolerance for my hunting was a general tolerance for the drive of a red-blooded male—not unlike if I was into Harleys or vintage Ford Mustangs or weightlifting or if I painted my face green and white on Sundays when the New York Jets played. She loved me and was willing to go along with my "hobby."

A week after the parental visit, we were in my truck headed south on New York's Route 88. Our destination was a kennel and breeder and trainer of English pointers in the Empire State's Southern Tier. From southwestern Vermont, where we lived at the time, the drive would be about three and a half hours. All to simply look at a dog I had no serious intention of buying—I had equipped myself with nothing for a puppy, not even a leash or water bowl. This was intended to simply be a fact-finding, window-shopping trip. C and I had talked about it, briefly, impetuously, but with no distinct plan about assimilating a pup into our family life.

I had spoken with the breeder's wife on the phone a few days earlier, asking whatever intelligent questions I could about dog lineage. "Are they Elhew pointers?" I led with. No, she said, not nearly as expensive, but from great genes nonetheless. The sire was indeed New York dog of the year according to one of the field-trial organizations, including National Amateur Pheasant Shooting Dog Champ on October 8, 1998. My notes tell me now that during the course of the conversation, dogs such as Red Water Rex and Mr. Awesome came up—whether or not they were related to the sire, Comanche's Tonto, or the dam, Midnight Delta Lady, I can't recollect. "Not run-away" is a phrase I wrote down twice during that phone conversation. The sire was a field-trial dog, so I surmised that it probably had long legs. Not really, she said. The pups were about ten or twelve weeks old; she couldn't remember the exact birth date. I took directions to a small town outside of Norwich, New York, and made an appointment to visit that weekend.

The dirt road that led to the kennel was the same as any dirt road in Vermont, or the one that led to my childhood home in central New York—potholed, lined by leafless maples and shaggy pines, cleared fields on one side, and some disabled farm machinery or vehicles settled into the weeds and merrily rusting. The house and attached kennel and outdoor dog pens were as gray as any December day was. There was no snow yet, which was a bit surprising for the time of the year. The driveway was muddy, and as we stepped out of the truck, the smell of dog waste was rather profound. I could see puppies in a pen at the back of the property. Several dogs were outside on chains; a few more were in the kennel stalls.

We made small talk with the breeder, who, as a student of animal behavior, knew right away, I have no doubt, that thin blond California girl C and I would be fine parents to one of his dogs. We walked back to the pen, C adroitly sidestepping the coils of crap mixed in with the mud.

There they were—nine writhing, mewing, yapping English pointer puppies. Ticked, liver spotted, some orange in their markings, some mostly liver and white. Crashing against the chicken wire, wrestling, pacing, and snarling—or seeming to snarl, because why would a puppy actually snarl?

I was attracted to the two orange-spotted twins in the litter we studied at Midnight Kennels. Loving the orange-spotted Nell, Brendan's dog, I was drawn toward that pair of pups—orange spots around one eye each, and orange ticking around their little white puppy-fat bodies. I had my mind made up. And then C pointed out that there was one crazy puppy up on its haunches and pleading for love. While the other pups scampered and whined, C had noticed one that sat on her haunches and stared at us.

"That's the one," the breeder said. "That's what I would take. Look at her high tail. Look at her markings. She's a classic pointer. I hate to give her up." I remember that fully, because it was such good advice of the brand that tends to stay with you through life, if you listen right.

She was good, this pup. She was confident, staring straight at us. She was more muscular already than the others, not so pudgy, not so wrinkled, though certainly both. The way she stared and shook with excitement told me she was fearless. She stood up and stared us down.

This little girl with a white body and floppy ears, liver spots ringing her eyes, and pink piggy nose kept staring—that's what she did. She stared me down. C knew, too, that this was our dog.

The breeder marked her with a tattoo on her right ear. "You don't want some asshole telling you your dog is his dog if she gets away from you," the breeder said. "Gotta have something to tell her by." The tat is of the number seven. I asked for five, but the breeder couldn't find that ingot for the tattoo handpress. So we went with seven, actually 07. She squirmed under the pressure of the press, and C squirmed at the sight of puppy blood oozing from the ear. The breeder got us a tissue and said, "Yer gonna be good parents; she's in good hands, this one. Yer gonna love her." And then, after I wrote a check for $300 (a bargain compared with the $500 asking price, because I came from Vermont, he said) and we scuffed mud and dog doo from the soles of our boots, we hopped in my pickup, with a puppy between us in the front seat.

I had no puppy accoutrements—no dish or collar or bones or toys or food, even. I had not thought that I would really buy a puppy. We had passed a Wal-Mart on the way to the breeder, so there we stopped on the way out of small-town Norwich, New York. Collar, munchy bones, Puppy Chow, a medium dog crate, several nylon leashes—it all put about $200 on my credit card. But I had a puppy in the front of my truck. She slept, on C's lap or the floor of the truck, the whole three hours home to Vermont—a curled-up white puppy with liver spots over her eyes. She snored as we hit the interstate, twitching from time to time. I thought, as I drove her to her new home, What was she dreaming? She would wake later, not to her mewling siblings, but to the embrace of two fawning adults intent on making this puppy their own. Oh, this little miss whitey dog . . .

That first night, I fed the dog and tried to settle her into the newly assembled plastic medium dog crate—"airline safe" the box said, which I suppose made me feel better about spending the $60 or $70 for it, just knowing that it would last the abuse of baggage control during airline travel, if I ever took the dog hunting out west. (Not a wish I wanted to share with C on the first night with our puppy.) Was it that night that we agreed to a name?

I said that, as C and I were both from Irish-American stock, the dog should be an Irish pointer and suggested Fergus from the Yeats poems, or maybe Joyce, after James. I joked that we could do O-Seven, after the dog's tattoo.

"Reilly," C said. She loved that name for a dog, she told me. Was there more to it? Had she secretly wanted a dog named Reilly from her adolescent days spent dressing up stuffed animals? I didn't care—I liked the name. I agreed.

"Reilly Joyce Healy!" I declared.

Now our dog had an identity to which she would respond. This is the first step in the long haul of training—choosing a name. Commands then follow, heel and whoa and come 'round and fetch— all to be preceded or followed by that name. Dog trainers often say that a one-syllable familiar name is best for a working dog, for the purpose of being declarative—"Come, Pep!"—when you call it. I never considered that; I liked Reilly too much.

"Well, Reilly, welcome to your new home," I said, scratching her ears and rubbing her pointy puppy tail. "And welcome to where you're sleeping tonight," I added, pointing to the plastic airline-safe kennel. I told C that our family had a golden when I grew up, and that she was a champion shedder and a ribbon winner at rolling in all manner of foul matter—rancid fish washed ashore on my home lake, putrid field mouse carcasses. I would never allow a dog into my bed; that kennel was for sleeping. "It's humane," I said. "Puppies like small enclosures. It's a womb thing." Imagine: I said that to a woman!

I tried to put Reilly-pup in the kennel. I had to push her in, which worried me that I would terrorize her and make her fear kennels the rest of her life, as if by throwing her in a pond I would be ruining her for water for the rest of her days. How do you get an unhousebroken dog into a plastic, steel-gated dog box bought at a discount department store? I helped her along, let me say, and turned out the light, thinking that she might weep but would eventually have to sleep. Before I made it through brushing my teeth, I already couldn't take the whining. Neither could C. She suggested we pull out the sofa in the living room and at least be close to our new Reilly; proximity would be a comfort was the theory.

What a setup! We pulled out the couch and made it up with bedding. I released Reilly and moved the kennel to the side of the convertible bed, and then reentered the dog to my vision of what a puppy's confined world should be. She whimpered, whined, wept, and cried. After about ten minutes, C told me that for the first night, we owed it to our dog to have her sleep with us and get to know our scent. That made sense—knowing our scent would make her less afraid, more assimilated into her new life.

Up she came, Reilly, her flaccid puppy body a bundle of our joy. Babies and puppies have a smell that makes us love them even beyond our adult attraction to the sight of them. Reilly's was sweet—some sawdust, still some faint fecal waft, some earthen dirt. Combine that with her heft—I called her my sack of potatoes—and I was happy to have her sleeping with us. She nestled between me and C, resting on both our legs, and we all bunched up into family sleep. The last I heard, Reilly was snoring evenly. I couldn't believe my luck.

Luck breeds paranoia, at least to an Irish Catholic trained on guilt and the eternal need for confession and redemption. I had put the dog in the crate. I had tried to make her suffer. I was guilty. I awoke from haunted dreams. The dog was pressed into the crease between me and C, outside the sheets, layered over us. I patted her, and she felt soft and cold. The woodstove was out; being December in our drafty carriage barn, it was cold inside. I pushed the dog. I pulled her. She didn't move. I shoved her in the ribs. I sat bolt upright. I had a thunderous realization.

"Holy hell! We killed her! Something's wrong. *Ohmygod . . . we gotta get a vet!*"

I was still half asleep and groggy. C rolled over and said "Wha?"

I lifted the dog under her midsection. She simply sagged. "Ohmygod!" I said. I thought of sudden infant death syndrome—somehow, by removing the dog from her littermates, from her brothers and sisters, she had suddenly died. Was it heartbreak?

As I lifted the dog higher in a sort of Hamlet-like dramatic effect, she shook her head and opened her eyes. She snorted, and C asked what the hell was wrong with me. I thought of a story I had read in the Minneapolis *Star Tribune* when I lived for a short time in Minnesota, about a parent who had drunkenly rolled on his children, suffocating them during sleep. I wasn't drunk—but was I a fit parent?

C told me to go to sleep; the dog was fine.

"We're going tomorrow and getting some books," I said, gently repositioning the dog into the crevice between our legs. "I have no clue about what to do with a dog. And I want to train her as a hunting dog? I can't even get her into her crate. And I almost killed her tonight."

C told me I had done no such thing. She asked me to kiss her. And then all three of us fell asleep, my hand resting, as it did most nights for the next seven months, half on Reilly and half on the bum of C.

CHAPTER 2

The Early Life of Reilly

THE NEXT MORNING, AFTER THE FIRST NIGHT OF GROUP SLEEP WITH C, me, and the pointer pup, I fed Reilly and took her out in the front yard for a while. She dragged a nylon leash but was otherwise unchecked. She was active and attentive, and I was astounded that she so quickly assimilated away from the kennel, the only home she had known for the ten short weeks of her life, as if she were ready to pounce into the larger world all in one huge stride. Talk about relation to awareness, as psychologists describe a child's awakening to the larger world around him. This was a puppy; where did the gumption come from? Was every dog this way, so well adjusted straight out of the kennel? Did I just get lucky? She even seemed to respond to her day-old name.

After I brought her back inside, I bundled her into the plastic crate in the kitchen, and C and I left for Northshire Books, in search of dog-training titles. Northshire is the best bookstore in southwestern Vermont, from sheer force of inventory, if not for the staff's keen sense of what inventory they should be keeping. I pushed my way through the holiday shoppers drawn to Manchester for its umpteen outlet stores, navigated the narrow passages between the book stacks, made it to the Pet section, and picked books amid the grab of three other shoppers hunched and studying the outward-facing spines on that rack. I was looking for one book in particular—not one of Richard A. Wolters's series, not one of Robert Wehle's classics (though I will write about the influence of Wehle's books on me), not any book specific to the training of working dogs or pointers. I wanted a puppy-training book, and the best I had heard of—from friends, from my research, and from a spirit of support for local achievers—was *The Art of Raising a Puppy,* by the Monks of New Skete.

In Cambridge, New York, about twenty or thirty minutes from Bennington, Vermont, is a monastery from behind the walls of which some of the country's best-bred and best-trained German shepherds spring. Monks, of course, have lots of time on their hands away from office meetings and conference calls, and now e-mail and Internet surfing, during which to focus on breadmaking and brewing and chanting and such. The Monks of New Skete make pies and dog biscuits and train dogs. They are brilliant in this regard. They raise good and great dogs. Obedient and well-adjusted dogs. And though I wasn't planning to take my pointer there for bird-dog training—the monks rarely take in outside dogs for training, I'm told—I was going to learn from their book.

The Art of Raising a Puppy is the best book I've found for first-time dog owners. In the first weeks during which I owned Reilly-pup, I clutched that book close to me, reading it with great fervor and acceptance—and frustration and disappointment about my outcomes. Most of all, it got me through one of the most difficult stages of training in puppyhood—housebreaking.

The monks call the process house-training, but I've always known it as housebreaking. Which I suppose is an idiomatic slip on my part. In dog-knowledge terms, house-training is the more accurate phrase for making your dog safe for human home life; housebreaking, and house-soiling, is actually what the dog does when you don't train it well. Reilly, I found as soon as I let her out of her crate on our return from the bookstore, saw hardwood floors as a convenient piddle platform. In the days to follow, a pool on the kitchen floor was no great surprise; indeed, it was expected. I whisked the dog out the door anytime she hunched into her poop stance, and I avoided most, though not all, carpet logs that way.

Like all dog training, house-training is achieved through repetition, as well as attention on your part. In the morning and evening, take the dog outside. Don't give it a reason to want to go number one or number two in the house. Don't leave it unattended for long spells. Keep it in the crate when you're not around.

I put Reilly in the crate when I was out of the house, though no more than three hours at a time, the absolute longest duration that was acceptable to the monks. I came home for lunch to let her out and left work early whenever I could to see that she was free before she had the urge to soil the crate, which she never did. This, I feel, made the crate a safe place for Reilly to this day. She never messed the crate and found its confines, if not comforting, at least tolerable.

This crate or kennel training was the first important training step, I found, to having a hunting dog in the house. Working dogs are generally high-energy, curious breeds that will chew, eat, or obliterate your household possessions, if given the chance. Crate training keeps them in check when they're young. Use the command "kennel" to introduce your dog to a crate. Years later, when you're hunting, you will want your wet and muddy dog to kennel when you tell it to. You will not want that dog on the bucket seat of your SUV. You will want it in the back, safe in its kennel. You can prepare for that need first thing in dog ownership by making the crate or kennel a familiar place.

How did I do it? I put an old T-shirt, one that I wore for a day of stacking wood and then did not wash so that it held my sweat and my scent, in the crate, and led her in while telling her to kennel. I also put a few toys in the kennel and rewarded her with a biscuit once I closed and locked the gate. After about three weeks, it started to work: She would go to the crate when I said, "Kennel." Would she whine a little? Yes, sure. But babies cry and dogs whine, and you just have to live with it. Both stop after a while, once they settle into the environment. You can tell quite clearly the pitch of distress from the call for attention, so don't fawn over a dog whining for attention. It'll stop. Don't give in.

In those first weeks of pet ownership, I also worked at the house-training system offered by the Monks of New Skete. House-training comes before bird-dog training—you can't have a house dog that's not trained to be a house dog, bird dog or otherwise. I'll give you a digested version of the monks' system; get their book for more. They point out that catching your dog in the act is the best way to control the act—any unwanted act, but this is most important with house-training. Vigilance is crucial. Don't let the dog have the freedom to soil the house.

The most intriguing part of the monks' system, to me, is using a trigger word to get the dog to go. To this day, I coax Reilly to "do it, do it" nearly every time we're outside and she's due to poop. The monks explained the importance of having your dog develop a consistent "elimination" schedule. When you're late for work and your dog still hasn't done her morning duty, you will wish you used this advice. It works. As when an outfielder says, "Swing batter," in Little League baseball as the pitcher delivers the ball, the words are intended to trigger action. The batter swings; the puppy poops.

In a way, encouraging your dog to eliminate is a cornerstone of obedience training. You want the dog to learn to eliminate on your schedule, not on its. Maybe it's the ultimate act of obedience. Otherwise, you load the family in the car and take off for the beach, and if the dog hasn't gone that morning, you will have a mound waiting for you when you get home sunburnt and tired. You're not happy, but neither is your dog, particularly if it went in its crate.

When you're training a pup for life and for hunting, this call-and-response method will make your life more manageable. It was the most important piece of advice I found in the monks' book, though the tome is loaded with good advice that will help you in important ways if you're a first-time dog owner. The book will make you more confident about owning a dog and about training it with satisfying results. Even if you kennel your dog 90 percent of the time, having it in the house untrained that other 10 percent could be unpleasant or even nightmarish. And what if you want to travel with the dog to grandma's house, or to a motel if you're on a hunting trip? House-train the dog.

After we had had Reilly six weeks, I found these training methods invaluable for stasis in the house. I also found myself less stressed out, because the dog was not complicating life for me by running willy-nilly around the house or by withholding her personal waste as I was trying to make a dinner reservation. This meant I was less prone to outbursts against the dog, which are not helpful in controlling or encouraging your young hunting dog's elimination habits. You'll have plenty of "Goddamn it!" moments later on during hunting training, believe me. Don't play those cards now, when your dog is young and formative. You want your dog to like you, to take to you. You want to play the alpha role in your dog's life. So treat it right.

A side note: As I was writing this, I heard the author Jon Katz on *Fresh Air,* hosted by Terry Gross on National Public Radio. Writing his book *The New Work of Dogs* led Katz, a certified dog trainer, to discover the advantage of crate training and how it will help in house-training by giving the dog a safe place in which to rest while you control its potty habits. He said he house-trained two dogs in a day each by feeding them in the crate, and then carrying them outside to poop. It works; I did it, too. Try it yourself.

Speaking of control, quite by accident, I developed a safety phrase that kept Reilly from running into the street and halted her when she ambled or sped off toward the woods. I had been relying on a simple restraint to keep Reilly close to the house: a fifteen-foot-long check cord attached to her collar. She did not go unsupervised, of course, but I could not have caught her if she decided to take out a red squirrel on a log in the field, whether she was dragging a long cord or not. An English pointer could give a greyhound a good chase. Worst of all would be if the red squirrel marked for death was at the edge of the far side of a road. A dog will not stop to watch for traffic as it heads to behead the red. This is how dogs are killed before they ever have a chance to show their hunting promise.

After I read from the monks about the persuasive power of "do it," I began to think about safe words I could use to make Reilly instantly stop doing what she was doing and respond to me. No, "Goddamn it!" did not work. Food did. And now, by simply shouting "Puppy Chow!" I can get her to stop chasing red squirrels and come to the front door. It helps to reinforce the command with some food, just a handful of kibble. She also comes to "treat," though not with quite so much Pavlovian fervor as she does for the former phrase. Develop your own safe phrase, whether it's "Puppy Chow" or "Euki" or "Iams" or "kibble" or "food" or "Mighty Dog"—or whatever. You can try "Goddamn it!" But that, in my opinion, will only confuse matters.

The rudimentary training persisted through Christmas, for which holiday I brought my girl Reilly home to meet my parents; C went to her family on the West Coast. My mother asked, before I drove home to central New York, "But will she curl up with me? That's what I want for Christmas. The puppy to curl up on my feet when I take a nap."

It was a Christmas of legend. Reilly kenneled on command; she eliminated outside my parents' house (well, there was some excitement pee once or twice), and with a ribbon on her collar, she became the Christmas pup. We had our usual decadence of beef filet and crab and lobster and martinis washed down with wines from my brother's cellar.

Next, Reilly was the Millennium pup. My parents, my brother, and I rented out a colonial bed-and-breakfast in Vermont for the year 2000 celebration, and though they didn't allow dogs inside, it was proximate to my house and we all spent lots of time with the dog as well as each other. In my journal from that year—which is quite full, actually, as I was writing a novel, editing a book, working on a live-in relationship with C, training the dog, editing a magazine for a day job, and keeping liner notes on all this along the way—the entry for New Year's is blank.

We had a good time, let's just say. I cooked in the B&B kitchen, and we ate crab cakes and crown roast, had fireworks the night of the dawning of Y2K, and drank lots of good wine, against which we balanced martinis and a crazy iced-tea drink that my brother's date introduced us to. Reilly was there the next morning to lick my head as it throbbed on New Year's Day of the one year in our lifetime ending with three zeros.

Later in January, on Martin Luther King weekend, my college roommate Mason and his girlfriend Cathy (now his wife and mother of three children) came to stay with me and C and Reilly in Vermont. Mason and I skied, and Reilly was in fine athletic form, jumping and romping on the pull-out couch as Mase and Cathy and C and I relaxed by the fire, but Reilly was still conforming to the house rules of no chewing and no tug-of-war, a terrible ethic that destroys the retrieving instinct in a hunting dog. She was going to the crate on the kennel command and responding to trigger words. When she pushed out the door and ran for the woods, "Puppy Chow" brought her around. I felt, if not the master of my domain, at least in a fair amount of control over my dog. But that feeling didn't last. Along came reality.

You will have disappointments when you own a pointing dog—that's a guarantee. I don't mean the general disobedience of the dog not coming to hand. Or the dog not holding to wing or shot. I'm talking about the dog eating the upper portion of a $250 Danner hunting boot or the heel of your $100 Nike cross-trainers. Or the dog chewing the first fifty pages of the collected works of William Butler Yeats.

So was my reality in January to March of 2000. The dog went haywire. Was she spoiled? Well, we had her spayed, and that could have caused a rebellion. Reilly seemed fine with the stitches; the two days at the vet's away from Mom and Dad were, I would guess, more traumatic overall for C and me than the surgery itself.

But C felt guilty and made Reilly her girlfriend, dressing her in scarves and things and brushing her teeth and bathing her and talking the baby talk, as in "Oh, Reilly-honey" and "You good, sweet baybee." Yup, the dog had her own way. This was particularly clear when I got back from a week away on business in Miami. When I got home, Reilly's coat smelled of perfume and her breath was minty fresh. A whole lot of pampering was going on.

We enrolled in obedience training at a kennel near our house but made the dog an obedience-school dropout when it was clear that sitting and staying were not commands I wanted to blend into a working dog's repertoire—nor did I want the dog to hyperventilate each session by being around other dogs with which she couldn't play, because this was obedience school and the rule was that there would be no roughhousing. C also wasn't crazy about the trainer, whom she thought was a bit overzealous in his discipline of dogs.

As the Vermont snow in the fields around my house decayed, and brown peeked through the withering crust of white, and the trees began to bud, and the buds led to leaflets, and the brown ground shaded to green, I looked beyond the monks to a reference geared more toward my dog-training needs. I looked to training sources for hunting dogs. The book at hand was *Pointing Dogs* by Kenneth C. Roebuck. It's a fine book, written in a breezy tone by an author who, although he lives in downstate New York, comes off as an eternal British gentleman. (I've never met the author; I learned he was born in Britain from the bio on the book jacket.) I was blown away by all that lay in front of me. I'd snap at C, "Don't bang pots around the dog!" because I was afraid that would make Reilly fear gunshots. When the dog ran straight away from me, always dragging a long check cord, I'd wonder when she'd be ready for whistle training. Steady to wing and shot was a sublimated worry compared to these surface concerns. How would the dog pattern? Would she stop at "whoa"? Would she run in the road and be dispatched by a rusted-out Plymouth?

The snow was gone from what had been a fairly snow-heavy Vermont winter, and to dismiss my flood of fears about all the ways in which I would screw up this perfectly capable, trainable hunting dog, I went to the section in the Roebuck book about the time-tested pointing-dog exercise called a-wing-on-a-string. Got a pointing dog? Wanna know if it points game? *Tro a wing at 'im!* This has been the long-standing gauge of whether your pointing dog will work. As the story goes, back in the truly competitive field-trial days, in the 1950s or thereabouts, when men had no remorse about their actions and were not in touch with their inner selves and had to do what they had to do, a puppy that did not respond to the wing-on-the-string test probably met its end so as not to taint the blood pool of that particular line. My uncles would have killed a dog if it didn't hunt, that I am sure of. They were practical Adirondack men who labored hard—and who did hard labor. My father, after getting his master's degree and starting life as a high school teacher, was less fierce. But I could see Uncle Mike or Uncle Gerry, as young men, putting puppies in a burlap sack and tossing it into the Black River because the dogs didn't hunt. I'm not saying this happened. But it could have.

A generation younger, and a self-abashed sensitive male, it didn't matter a whole lot to me whether the dog responded to the wing test; she would be a part of the family whatever her avian inclinations. So the wing test it would be. Roebuck writes:

> A bird wing, which can be that of a quail, a pheasant, a duck, or a pigeon, as examples, is attached to the end of a fishing line; then, allowing for sufficient length of line, the fishing pole is held at such an angle that the wing just touches the ground. When the puppy is running loose, the wing is jigged around slightly while he's looking in the right direction. This will certainly arouse the pup's interest; he will probably stop, look, then dash in to grab it. But make sure he doesn't get his mouth on it. Do this by whipping the wing up and away in time; this is important.

That was a great passage to read about early bird training, I felt. I asked my friend and colleague Larry Kenney to send me a couple pheasant wings from a hunt near his house in Oregon with his two springer spaniels. When they arrived, I tied them to a 10-pound-test leader attached to the line on a 5-weight fly rod. I tossed, I jigged, I jammied, I farandoled. I capered. I did the fandango while lopping the wing all over the lawn. I did the hustle. I shook my own tail feather as I stripped the wing for the pup to see.

Reilly, the entire time, throughout my demented dance steps, held a low-tailed point. I repeated these theatrical actions. She crept some as I brought the wing closer to her, but I said nothing, gave no commands. And she held her own unschooled version of a point. For a while, at least. And then she pounced for the wing-on-a-string, and I lifted it up and away. I did the exercise about four times and then stopped. I had learned what I wanted to learn. The hereditary gene was activated on that day: Reilly was a pointer, and evidence indicated that she would point birds for me.

CHAPTER 3

An Introduction to a Professional Hunting-Dog Trainer

In March of 2000, having negotiated a new position for myself with the magazines I worked for, I bought (through a large pay cut) more time away from the office. This, I hoped, would allow me to finish a novel I was writing and to begin to train Reilly with proper attention. But away from work, I became confounded to the point of being mildly immobilized about dog training. I had covered what the monks taught in print; I had read and studied and reread what I considered to be a helpful pointer-training book by Kenneth Roebuck but had stalled with that guide after hitting the chapter called "Faults." Would I ruin Reilly's tolerance if I shot a gun near her? Would I destroy her staunchness by letting her munch one of my mooched pheasant wings? And how the hell could I ever quell the affliction of pointing dogs called *blinking,* otherwise known as a demonstrative lack of interest in pointing game?

I talked to Brendan Banahan, and he suggested I call a trainer just getting established with his kennels across the border from Vermont near the village of Cambridge, New York. This trainer, Brendan told me, was an acolyte of one of the great pointing-dog trainers (specializing in weimaraners) of the 1970s and '80s. The Cambridge area, including Manchester, Vermont, and around the Batten Kill corridor of Route 313, was the home of many active sportsmen during the mid to late twentieth century. Less than four hours from New York City, yet knocking on the door of the Adirondacks and the Green Mountains, and home to great trout fishing on the Batten Kill and upland bird covers holding woodcock and grouse, the area attracted a gathering of sportsmen of the time, such as Burton Spiller and Corey Ford and even, for a time, fly-fishing great Lee Wulff. That the Orvis Company had headquarters in Manchester helped attract this sporting tropism to the area through the decades, and still does to this day. The bird hunting there is challenging today, however, as coverts have been cleared to make way for development, and the fishing in the Batten Kill is difficult. As I write this in late 2003, close to a million federal dollars have been apportioned and poured into Batten Kill research, the goal of which is to determine the cause of the decline in the river of brown trout—a foreign species to begin with, as German brown trout have been stocked from foreign sources and are nonnative throughout this country.

Brendan had bought a country house in Cambridge when he lived in New York City in the late 1980s and had quickly assimilated into the sporting culture, largely through the encouragement of his uncle Dick, who had retired to that part of New York. Dave Slohm, who had managed the gun department at Orvis for years, was another influence in his bird-hunting education. Brendan's pointer, Nell, led to his acquaintance with Chet Cummings, who agreed to evaluate Nell when she was a puppy and eventually to train her.

I wish I had met and known Chet; the closest I came to that was waving to him and his wife, Ginger, from the front seat of Brendan's Explorer as he kenneled Nell at Chet's farm before we tore off for a weekend of fly fishing on the beaches of Cape Cod in the late 1990s. Chet was one of the country's top dog trainers in the later twentieth century, scoring his greatest acclaim with his dog Fritz von Weimar, a weimaraner national champion field-trial hot rod. Chet himself had moved to the New York–Vermont border area from Litchfield, Connecticut.

"I first met Chet in 1982, and we brought two dogs back in then. They were setters. Chester trained weimaraners. I asked him why, and he said, basically, 'Those are the only people who have money,'" Jeff Gaess told me. Jeff had dogs trained by Chet and eventually bought Chet's farm in Greenwich, New York. "We had a lotta great years until his passing. He was very particular with what he did. That was his whole life. He told me that he was hunting with his father and his uncle when he was ten years old, and I think one of his uncle's friends had a dog. And that dog went on point. They flushed the bird and shot it, and Chet said from that point on is when he decided he wanted to be a dog handler."

The trainer Brendan suggested for Reilly had taken over Chet's kennels after he died, while Jeff Gaess was figuring out the closing on the farm with Chet's family. The trainer, who had worked with Chet for years, was John Offerman, a German shorthair owner who shared my passion for pointing dogs and who came to love my dog as I do.

John and I did not become fast friends during our first meeting one day in June. At first we had a business relationship. He began by asking me what results I wanted from my dog, and I said, "To draw the best of her instincts out." After a brief lawn assessment of Reilly's degree of performance at the nine-month stage, he told me directly that to get the results I wanted, it would be best to kennel Reilly with him full-time. I didn't blink. I had asked my friend Larry Kenney, an Oregonian whose springer spaniels were professionally trained, "Do they still know you when they get back from a summer in a kennel?" He gave me the most persuasive advice I had received at that point in my early life as a pointing-dog owner: "Well, after a couple months at the trainer's, Feather [one of Larry's springers] ran into the house, jumped on the couch, and looked at me like, 'What's up, Dad?'"

So I wouldn't kill my relationship with my young dog by leaving her with a trainer.

Larry continued on a positive note: "My springers live for human attention as much as they do for birds. One of the underacknowledged advantages of placing a dog with a pro trainer is that the dog gets a maximum amount of human attention during training and not much attention at other times. Gone too are the confusing signals that come from a devoted owner and his family. My male pup knew from experience that I wasn't all business; fifteen minutes with the trainer and he knew he wasn't going to get away with anything. At the trainer's, nothing else during the day was a tenth so interesting as when the guy with the hat opened the kennel door and took him to the training field. A dog in this situation is eager and focused and, I suspect, learns better."

I asked John whether he would mind if I joined in the training, to get a rudimentary knowledge of what he would be doing with the dog. He told me it would be no problem, and we agreed to a summer-long price of about $900 for training and boarding.

So on the Fourth of July weekend of 2000, on the way to central New York to spend the weekend at the lake on which my parents lived, C and I dropped off Reilly at John's comfy heated kennels, with cedar chips in each dog box. We told the ten-month-young puppy that she was in good hands. C cried. I almost did. But fifteen minutes later, we were free from the rigors of owning a young dog. And I couldn't wait to get back to the kennel to watch John train her.

CHAPTER 4

Mornings with John Offerman
Learning His Training Plan

"The formula for getting a dog to perform to its best abilities is 'genetics plus training plus nutrition.'"

—*George Hickox*, Shooting Sportsman,
January–February 2004

As I drove up the winding dirt driveway to the kennel that July morning, eight o'clock news on the truck radio, my window down, and a travel mug of coffee in my hand, I heard the howl.

"*OOOOHHHAAWWLLLLAAOOLLL . . .* " Reilly could not see my truck from her kennel stall; did she recognize the gear-train noise of the Toyota, the only truck she'd ever ridden in, beginning the day we brought her home from the breeder? Did she somehow *smell* my approach? How could she know I was nearing the kennel? I did not ask John about that. When I got out, he was hosing down a kennel. He didn't extend his hand for a shake. He seemed pissed—which I quickly surmised had to do with my arriving about ten minutes past eight, putting him off schedule for the morning walk.

"We usually start the walk right at eight," he flatly said, curling up the green garden hose.

I apologized, swished my toe in the grass like a kid, took off my ball cap, and scratched my head.

The walk, I found out, was a mile-and-a-half loop around the property on which John Offerman would be conducting his summer-long pointer-dog training on a cut trail so that the dogs could run ahead and check back with us. The dogs, and John, could stretch their legs, socialize, and get the day started. I saw that John was not so much pissed as he was irritated not to be started on the routine on schedule. Much of dog training—the foundation of the training, I would come to learn that summer—is about sticking to routine. "I cannot over-emphasize the importance of consistency," Robert G. Wehle writes in *Wing & Shot*. "Inconsistency will not only make the training job extremely unpleasant for both you and your dog, but it will also make it a much longer and more laborious task than is necessary."

We walked in silence for the first hundred yards or so, Reilly leading the pack, which consisted of John's German shorthair, Bo; three English setters owned by Jeff Gaess; and Jeff's house dog, a snippy Jack Russell mix named Britta that was fixated on Reilly. John told me he was keeping a close eye on Bo and one of Jeff's setters, TJ, as the two males had been squaring off recently. A small, orange-marked setter bitch, Tabasco, was my immediate favorite; she was about Reilly's size, around thirty-six pounds, though years older than Reilly's ten months. Younger was Tully, another setter bitch of affectionate demeanor. The dogs bounded off into the new summer's hay, Reilly flailing with her front paws as if swimming through the tall grass.

"Looks like she's doing the breaststroke," I said to John, and we both laughed.

"She's a good girl, that Riles," he said. Already she was nick-named. He told me that exercise was a key part of controlling a high-strung breed like a pointer. "Got to wear down their batteries." Reilly fit the definition of a "nervous energy" dog of the kind so preferred by master pointer breeder and trainer Robert G. Wehle. In his book *Snakefoot: The Making of a Champion,* about his national champion pointer Elhew Snakefoot, Wehle writes, "It is so exciting to develop a young dog with a high degree of energy. It's a real challenge to bring out all the qualities of this dog without inhibiting his spirit or personality." Indeed, he credits English pointers with having a level of get-up-and-go hunting exuberance—or tenacity, as he prefers to call it—unmatched by other pointing breeds.

John stopped on our walk to explain that getting to the farm at eight o'clock, if I intended to keep coming on the morning walks and subsequent training, was not negotiable, particularly as the summer wore on; otherwise, the heat of the day impeded good training. The dew would burn off by ten or so, drying up bird scent, and by eleven it would be too hot for the dogs to be in the training field. (John called this field "the orchard," a romantic name that belied the fact that it had no fruit-bearing trees.) The heat was not good for the quail, either, the bird species he used in the field training.

"I guess I need training, too," I said, and he nodded. If John were a higher-octane personality, he would have high-fived me on that observation. It was the truest statement I could have made at that point. I knew next to nothing about the process on which we were embarking. I did feel comfortable that John knew what to do. On that morning, I saw that he was firm with the dogs, but not overly vocal or reproachful. "Come," "whoa," and "heel" were his main commands. When the dogs got out of sight in the woods during our walk, he wouldn't shout their names; he would simply wail, *"Heee-Uht"* to turn the pack toward us. I asked why.

"All's they need is the sound of your voice, just to let them know where you are." He would cup a hand to the side of his mouth, so that his call projected toward the dogs, and shout, *"Heee-Uht."* On cue, ringing bells would head our way. Reilly, in the company of the other dogs, was perfectly happy to wear a bell. I had tried putting one on her that spring, and she cowered at the sound or the weight around her neck. So I stopped trying, afraid that I would ruin her on the bell the way you can ruin a dog to the gun by introducing loud noises in inappropriate settings, or so I had read in various training books. I observed that first morning that the walk was a type of field training to accommodate the dogs to the bell, which I planned to use when hunting Reilly, as I liked the sound of the bell in the woods; some bird hunters use electronic beepers, which I find distracting and unnatural. It was also clear to my untrained mind that John was training the dogs to check back to the hunter/master as the morning walk unfolded.

After the walk—never much of a morning person, I now found this morning ritual enlivening—John led the dogs back to their kennel stalls and gave me a quick tour of the grounds. He wouldn't work the dogs on birds today, he said; he would rest them. We walked over to the quail pen, a two-by-four-foot chicken-wire cage with birds huddling in the corners. The cage was perched on legs to hold it about three feet off the ground so that coyotes and foxes and raccoons—and the dogs—couldn't get at the captive birds. Later he would move the pen to the training orchard.

"About the birds . . . " I began. I had thought about John using quail and had convinced myself that this seemed, well, out of place in the training of a woodcock and grouse dog. "What about, say, chukar or even pigeons?" I asked. "Aren't they closer to grouse than a quail, which I will probably never hunt with Reilly?"

John said that we were introducing the dog to bird scent, and it didn't matter which bird was used. Quail are economical, he said—they covey together at night, so after being planted and flushed, most would return each night to the pen, which had a funnel that let the birds reenter. "Quail believe in safety in numbers," he told me.

In a few weeks, closer to the end of August, he would begin shooting birds over Reilly, he said, and he would have to charge me up to $10 per bird. I told him I understood; I could use the feathers in fly tying. I also said that I'd never shot a quail, and maybe he'd give me a chance to shoot too.

"Oh, you can count on that," he said.

He then asked me why I had Reilly's name on her collar. "If she runs from you," he said, "do you want anyone else to know her name? Wouldn't they probably feel a whole lot more guilty about keeping her if your name and phone number were there on her collar?"

On my next visit to John's kennel, I brought along a new collar with an ID band on it bearing my name and not my dog's.

CHAPTER 5

First-Year Pointer Training Begins in Earnest

FROM THE DAY IN EARLY JULY WHEN I LEFT REILLY AT THE KENNEL, John and I had grown toward an understanding that I would shadow him in his training methods when I could. In return, I felt that he appreciated having a protégé following along with all he had learned from Chet. I told John, straight up, that I wanted to learn from him—enough that I would be confident about carrying on the dog training he was beginning that summer, which I knew would need to be maintained to keep the dog learning moving forward. I told John I would be deferential to what he told me.

Looking back, it was the right way for our relationship to begin. Don't we all have a tropism toward sharing what we know? Isn't that an ennobling part of the human spirit? John Offerman wanted to share with me what he knew about dogs. No, John wanted to train this dog to show what he knew about dogs. But he also wanted me to learn enough about the training that I could be a happy companion to this natural-born hunting machine that I called my pointer, Reilly. The teacher-pupil relationship, our common understanding of roles, hastened our path to friendship.

I knew my role; John knew his. And as he had learned about dog training from Chet Cummings, John was now willing to pass along a part of that knowledge to me. For a price, mind you. All told that summer, I shelled out about a grand to John: $300 a month training time, plus birds shot over the dog. But by the time I brought Reilly home on September 21, she was a changed puppy.

By mid-July, John had started Reilly on barrel or table training: putting her up on a table to keep her steady to the "whoa" command while stroking up her tail to introduce style, the preferred stance for Reilly's English pointer breed being pointing with tail held high; this was also holding her stable so she would learn to keep steady as she pointed birds for real in the field. Bob Wehle and his wife, Gatra, called this benchwork. He writes in *Snakefoot:*

> Any bench will do just so long as when a dog is standing on it his eyes meet yours. We use a conventional tool box that fits on the back of a standard pickup truck. This is mounted on a heavy wooden frame with a step at each end. I start very early coaxing them up, using the step, with a treat. When they are up I give them more treats and hug them a bit. They soon learn to climb up by themselves and really love to be there not only for the treats, but I believe for the eye contact and the proximity to me.

Off the table, in the training orchard, John was gently introducing Reilly to quail by letting her explore around the quail pen so she could gather bird scent.

John, or most likely Chet Cummings before him, had cleared a cross-hatch of paths into the one- or two-acre training field above the farm. The dogs could run on these paths while scenting the birds hand-planted in the thicker brush; near the old cemetery stones in that field, John (or Chet) had driven stakes so that we could pin down the two or three dogs from the kennel that we took up to the orchard, keeping those bullpen dogs in check while the starting dog was in training.

Reilly would wait as Bo or one of the English setters, Tabasco or Lady, or a visiting dog (of which there were a few that summer, Brittanys and shorthairs) was put through the paces to point a single bird or several quail that John had planted in the field.

Here's how bird planting of training quail works: John would slap his ball cap against the quail cage till a few birds were funneled toward the release hatch; then he would grab a butterfly net, open the hatch, and scoop out a few flapping protesters. Next, he'd pick some spots in the puckerbrush in which to drop birds; he'd mowed the field to varying levels of density so that he could put birds in varying degrees of cover. To plant a bird, simply tuck its head under its wing (seemed as though John always used the right wing) and shake the bird up and down the way you would a mustard jar, to disorient the bird so that it wouldn't fly away, and then firmly place it under some weedy brush. The bird now will hold till the presence or pressure from the dog in training flushes it—or till you have to apply a modicum of a toe push to get it in the air as the dog has established point.

Like many outdoor endeavors—fly tying and fly casting come to mind—this act of training is ritualistic in nature. Cause and effect. And repetition. You just keep trying. You plant the birds, release the dog—in young Reilly's case, on a long check cord so we could stop her from nabbing the birds—wait for the point, step in to flush the bird, pull away or call off the dog when the bird alights, shoot a starter's pistol, and hold the dog by the cord as the bird soars off into the neighboring cornfield. John Offerman and I must have done this one hundred or more times that summer. At least.

We became good friends, John and I. We became hunting friends and dog-loving friends. Those are huge bonds we shared—passions for hunting and dogs. John was a good friend. I miss him.

John was from New York, originally from Long Island. He had lived in California for a while and hated it, he told me. He was injured in an industrial accident while working on Long Island and had a bad back. A heavy barrel had fallen on him while he was off-loading it from a truck while working in salvage, severely damaging his verte-brae. As a friend, I never asked him to elaborate on the nature of his injury, though as a journalist, I was curious to know the details. The details were the reason he had come to the New York–Vermont bor-der area to train dogs. He needed a place to recuperate, had family in the area, and yearned for a slower pace of life. Now he wanted to ded-icate his life to training hunting dogs. "To the Point," John told me on one of our morning walks, would be the name of his new business.

We promised each other on one walk that we would hunt together in South Dakota and Montana. I had connections through the fly-fishing magazines with outfitters out west, and I told him that I'd look into that next year. He mentioned a trip under way for the Adirondacks and then told me that was probably something that only the members of the local hunting club would be invited to. Reilly wouldn't be ready for that, but maybe in a year a two we'd go out west. I told John that I'd teach him fly fishing if he gave me a break on dog training the next summer. Fly fishing was something he'd never done but wanted to try. You bet, he said.

Free of the responsibilities of having a puppy, my girlfriend C and I traveled that summer around the state of Vermont, to the islands up north on Lake Champlain and around the mountains of Manchester, me with a weather eye out for grouse and woodcock cover. C had some flexibility in her job as a social worker, and I had lots of flexibil-ity with my amended working hours, so every weekend that summer we planned a trip. We missed Reilly, the white puppy, but knew she was getting the training she needed with John. She was on birds every day. Repetition, repetition, repetition.

CHAPTER 6

Reilly and Me on the Road

ON ROUTE 67 ONE LATE MORNING THAT SUMMER, JUST AS I WAS DAY-dreaming about ordering my usual two-eggs-and-bacon-and-home-fries breakfast at Benson's Diner outside of White Creek, New York, after a morning working at the farm with John and Reilly and watching the dog tremble and shake but hold tight as a planted quail hunkered low in the thick grass a foot from her nose—the dog agitated but not breaking point, an action that spelled the beginnings of her pointing instincts being drawn out through the field training—I saw an image straight out of my dreams. Up on a knoll on the north side of the road, parked on the lawn that tumbled down from a tidy yellow farmhouse, sunlight glinting off its white aluminum siding, was a vintage green-striped vision sitting on two wheels, with its tongue leveled on a split piece of log: It was the single-axle travel trailer I had always wanted.

Ah, did my want for self-contained freedom run deep. Growing up, family vacations often found us in a musty, leaky, heavy, and hard-to-erect Coleman canvas-and-aluminum-poled tent. Inside, we slept on canvas bunk-bed cots. In musty, lumpy Coleman sleeping bags. If you had to pee at night, you rolled off the creaky cot and peed in a coffee can, the tinkle on tin a better option than waking the rest of the family with the rip of the tent zipper as you tried to get free of the tent. If you could get free, that is: Finding the well-concealed zipper tab was not easy, and the only source of illumination in the tent, the white-socked Coleman gas lantern, was verboten for us kids to handle; only Dad could work that potential Molotov lantern. (Fearing late-night laser-light-show fights between my brother and me, my parents would not give us flashlights.) So I would tactically feel for the coffee can, hold it close below the waist, lower the front of my pj's, and go, keeping the stream against the side of the can to avoid reverberation. I can't say I'm bothered by that memory today. But as an adult, I was no longer going there. We can be a bit more civilized in our leisure time, no?

A travel trailer meant a bathroom, beds, kitchen, fridge, lights, heat, radio, and possibly television. A new age in camping, in other words, from my primitive childhood camping experience. A mobile bird camp. An attack craft. The Grouse House.

For about two weeks, I made that drive along New York's Route 67 and projected myself into the interior of that travel trailer when I passed by on the commute to and from Reilly's training farm. There it was on the side of the road. Oh, if it had been sold, and not to me! My thinking was two-sided: On the upside, it was there, available, and on the road to Reilly, making it a clear karmic match; on the downside, the thing easily was at least at the limits of the hauling capacity of my Toyota Tacoma, if not heavier. I would amend my vision to that of one of those little bulbous-looking Scamps or something—a light, towable appendage to my truck. Then again, I would remind myself that I had C and Reilly to think about. A cubbyhole wouldn't do—I needed a mobile unit; a camper; a roving home.

So I stopped on my way to the farm one morning. I looked at the trailer. The door was open. Quietly, I entered. A table and an oven range. No shortage of storage cupboards. A fridge. A corner door that, when opened, revealed a toilet and shower curtain. I realized I'd be late for the morning walk with the dogs, so I bailed and drove to my training session with John. When I pulled down the dirt road to the farm, I saw that John was already winding up the hose after spraying down the kennel stalls—next would be the walk.

I jumped out of my truck, went to the back, lowered the tailgate, sat and pulled on my rubber muck boots. After the first week of walks with John in hiking boots, I learned that he wore rubber boots to the knee for a reason: to keep from soaking his pants with dew, and because the bottoms were easy to hose when you inevitably stepped in dog dirt. John wore nice green rubber Orvis or something boots; I bought mine at the now-defunct Ames store in Bennington for $12. I still wear them when training and hunting with Reilly, five years later.

I joined John just as he was releasing the dogs. After our morning handshake, we began up the first hill on the dog trail, and I began telling John my plan about the travel trailer.

"Jeez, that's something," he said. "Where you gonna take that?"

I told him the Adirondacks, northern Vermont, New Hampshire, Maine—hell, South Dakota and Montana, I said, carried away, I suppose, by my trailer exuberance and my romantic notion of rural space that was only being fueled by this walk through a gorgeous spread of land in upstate New York, with my hardworking pointer bounding through tall grass and then joining the pack to romp with beautiful setters, a clique of supermodel dogs if ever I saw one.

I told John I'd fix the damn thing up as much as it needed, but that it didn't need much work. "It's got electricity, clearly, off the battery and a power cord hookup. Running water with a john and a shower. An oven, with a rangetop, a fridge. It sleeps at least five!" I could smell the mustiness of the 1970s upholstery when I went inside. I could feel the floor rocking as I pushed from side to side, tipping the chassis back and forth on the two wheels. I could see the sun through the crank-turn skylight. A 1972 Open Road travel trailer, seventeen and a half feet, I learned from the sheet that was taped to the door.

On the way home from the farm, I stopped again. The idea was growing in my psyche.

Later, I asked Phil Monahan, a friend and editor from the fly-fishing magazine group, to come with me to give me an honest opinion. He liked what he saw. The interior was rough in some areas, he agreed. Ultimately, he could feel my excitement and told me it looked like a winner. Phil and his wife, Mary Beth, moved to Vermont from New Jersey to join our small publishing group. A small-town guy by nature, raised in New Hampshire, though educated at Columbia and later Rutgers, Phil had taken to rural Vermont quickly. He understood my yearning for a mobile camp. I knew I would soon own a trailer.

That night, I told C all about it. Funny, I never asked her to come look at it with me. Then again, it was my project; it was a project that fit hand-in-glove with my plans for Reilly.

Why, in a book about dog training, is there so much mention of a camping trailer? It was part of my dog plan, truly: Having a "brag dog," as the old-time trainers called the good working dogs, would mean hunting this dog, which would mean we'd be traveling wherever possible to follow the bird seasons. A trailer would go behind me to the Midwest, to pay an unannounced call to author Jim Harrison and his upland-hunting troupe gallivanting around the Upper Peninsula of Michigan. Through my editorship of *Saltwater Fly Fishing*, I had published a small excerpt from Harrison's *A Good Day to Die*; I feel fortunate to have had some semblance of contact with him, as I admire his work and was thrilled to share his words about fly casting for tarpon with our readers. Jim Harrison is also a bird hunter. In his worthwhile book *Making Game*, Guy de la Valdene wrote: "Jim and I hunt, a few times each season, a very special place, a place that every year draws an unrivaled and rotating supply of woodcock and by the looks of the cover will continue to do so for a long time. It is a place that we don't discuss in public, and it may be one of the only secrets either of us has ever kept."

We have evidence that Jim Harrison is a lover of hunting dogs from his autobiography *Off to the Side*. His dogs are mentioned throughout. "We in the Midwest have to face up to the idea that no one in America's dream coasts will visit us except for very special occasions." So wrote Jim Harrison. What more special occasion than bird hunting? In my scenario, I would make a grand visitation in my mobile hunting home with hunting dog and 12-gauge.

When I lived in Minnesota for almost a year, the one vast great emptiness was not having a hunting dog—cheated from exploring the available pheasant range, I was. I did hunt one afternoon with my colleague Kurt's brother, who had a fine pointing Lab. In a sorghum patch about an hour or so south of the Twin Cities, we trundled through gummy mud fields after pheasants, the only cock of which offered a hovering death shot yet surprised me so that I fumbled with the safety knob and whiffed miserably as the bird clacked and wing-beat to freedom.

A wild pheasant—an exotic creature I hadn't seen since I was about ten years old. My father and I had hunted together, and he shot at a bird not planted by the New York game and fish department that year, but surely a progeny of that stocking program at some point. He missed while I hit the deck in the brier patch from which I had flushed that tight-sitting bird, scared by the gun's percussion. I was too young to carry a gun and had not shot one yet. I was in the woods that day only as my dad's flushing boy. We had wild pheasants around my house while I was growing up in central New York, but today they're long gone from that neighborhood. So I hatched the dream of hunting with Reilly in the Midwest, the two of us and my trailer, set-tling for the season where fields were still tilled and game birds still wild.

I wanted to get back to the Midwest, courtesy of trailer empow-erment, with my dog. Camping by any roadside—hell, I had seen pheasants graveling along I-90 in South Dakota as I drove to Min-nesota from Jackson and Yellowstone one August week after I had arrived in and bailed out of Sturgis, South Dakota, during the annual Harley rally. Pheasants, pheasant, pheasants—green-headed birds strutting along the interstate's shoulder. Hunting in any likely field was my plan, pulling over, suiting up in brier gear, taking the gun from the back of my truck, releasing the dog, and following birds.

No doubt this vision of hunting in the West was a fantasy born from fly fishing, a sport that enables one to simply pull over and fish access areas while driving in any midwestern state. I'd have my trailer behind my truck, and riding shotgun in my truck would be young Reilly, all jacked up on nervous energy, with whom I would go from Vermont to I-90 through New York along the southern Great Lakes path to Ohio and Illinois and points west.

I got the trailer, but I never did the rest. Or I should say, I haven't yet. But what the trailer did for me was make me want to go. That was the promise it held—becoming a Tin Can Traveler, for the purposes of bird hunting with my little white-and-liver pointer through the country's open spaces—surely not as vast as they once were but still as necessary.

I haven't gone yet—but I will.

CHAPTER 7

Using a Check Cord to Break the Breaks

BUYING A 1972 TRAVEL TRAILER INVESTED IN ME A SENSE OF WANDER-lust. Having a pull-behind cabin made me think more than ever of how accessible this country is by roadway. I began rereading Steinbeck's *Travels with Charley* straightaway.

I finished *Travels* on a plane to Minneapolis, on another research trip for my work-in-progress novel, this time to South Dakota. The travel trailer needed cosmetic body work and the electric brake system checked and wasn't ready for this ramble, though I would have enjoyed the over-the-road travel a hell of a lot more than flying from Albany, New York, to Detroit to Minneapolis, via three airports each way. I drove a rental car from the Twin Cities to the Black Hills, out to Devils Tower and Belle Fourche, and returned through the Badlands, getting back to reality, as they say, by way of a night in Sioux Falls for a shower, a good walleye meal, and a bed after camping all the other nights. Then it was on to the Twin Cities to fly home. I was gone for five days and missed the farm and Reilly and C more than I ever anticipated.

When I returned, it was August, the second month of our first training year. John's aim each day was to bring Reilly to two or three quail (not too many, so as not to confuse her with a scent bath) that he had taken from the pen and planted in the grass and goldenrod. I'll never shake the image of gentle John flapping his ball cap toward the quail to usher a few over to the hatch so he could grab them; it reminded me of catching frogs when I was a kid.

After planting the birds, John held Reilly on a check cord hitched to her studded training collar, letting her range a bit around the orchard till she caught bird scent and then followed it to its source. When she was visibly birdy, John tightened the lead or check cord and softly talked to her to calm her by saying, under his breath, "Find the bird Reilly; hunt it up." He didn't chant this as a mantra—it's not good to distract a bird dog that's caught scent, he told me—but to reinforce and channel her behavior. When she got close to the bird, he would say, "Whoa," once—and only once, he made a point of telling me, a point we covered nearly daily during the training.

Probably the most damaging offense in dog training is a multiple, repetitive command—a verbal string like "Murphy, come; Murph, Murphydog, c'mon, come here. Mister Man, come, Mister Murphy, get over here! Come, come, Murphy, dammit, come!" This verbal spillage gets worse, I've observed, when a car approaches and the dog is near a roadway—yells, screaming, imploring. But it's better if the dog has been properly trained to come to begin with. Repetitive yelling of this sort only confuses the dog. It's lost in a soup of words. When you're dealing with tight tolerances to produce a specific effect or result, such as holding steady and not rushing in on a pointed bird, multiple, repetitive commands give a dog way too much leeway. There's no firm command to which it can respond. Better to say simply, "Murphy—whoa!" in a firm, decisive manner, not shouted or imploring.

Training Reilly to respond to one-word commands was one of the major goals that summer. As John walked her to a bird, she pulsed this way and that, scribing an arc controlled by the check cord, with John loosely steering in the right direction. She was now pointing hot and heavy, locking up tight once the scent was strong. John would softly say, "Whoa," and creep forward to her off-bird haunch, where he'd push on her back or behind—the idea being that pushing a pointing dog toward the source of scent will only increase its need to point that scent—and stroke up her whippy pointer tail. Then he'd motion for me to walk, slowly so as not to distract or agitate her, toward the bird. I'd begin to kick at the brush, John nodding toward the spot where the bird was stationed. Two, three kicks and the bird was airborne—and so was Reilly. So bottled up was her desire that she would launch herself right after the bird. But John held the check cord firm, causing Reilly to buckle backward when she broke and leapt. The goal here, he told me, was to break her from breaking—the first stage of steady-to-wing training.

When Reilly finally learned not to break, when she stood steady to the bird on the wing, John would shoot a starter's pistol just as the bird leveled off in flight, holding the pistol behind his back so the dog couldn't see it but only heard its *pop*.

He explained that because Reilly was so intent on following or chasing the bird, the gun report was just a background noise and didn't represent any threat to her. It was in this way that he acclimated her to the gun. It was effortless, really.

I'd heard stories about people banging pots and pans to introduce loud noises to their pups in simulation of gun reports. I've heard them talk about this strategy, dog owners proud that they'd toughened up their puppy even before taking it to the field. But from what I've learned from professional dog trainers and umpteen books on the subject, the pots and pans are better left in the pantry—this method often results in a dog that becomes shaky when hearing any loud noise, if not outright ruined to gunshots altogether. Get a starter's pistol and introduce it the same way you introduce birds—with moderation, at a pace that allows the dog to take in the stimulus unhurriedly and without fear.

Dogs are sensitive and can easily become fearful. Time and again, I've seen a dog lower its eyes and hang its head or, worse, outright cower because it's fearful of the possible negative results from an unexpected or unpleasing behavior. Honestly, Reilly has had her moments. She sometimes pisses me off to this day, that beautiful blockhead.

One reason I have never regretted my decision to give up my dog for her first summer to a dog trainer was that John Offerman didn't use electronic collars. The worst "shocks" Reilly received leading up to her first birthday were from the dull-tipped spikes on the inside of the training collar pressing into her neck or the restraint of the check cord pulling her off her feet if she broke after a bird—or a chipmunk or squirrel, for that matter. Reilly's first dog-training months didn't involve an electronic collar at all, and I believe that helped her continue to grow within the scope of her own nature and not be reduced to acting in any way simply to protect herself from the enforcement of the collar.

John Offerman didn't believe in using electronic collars; Chet Cummings had taught him never to rely on what John called "that crutch." So Reilly was trained using the relatively old-time method of being bowled over by a tug on the check cord if she broke on a bird she had pointed. Often this tug pulled her right back over herself. That went from happening on every bird in mid-July, to happening once a day in late July into August, to once a week.

This is prefacing information, because now I have an electronic collar on her much of the time. It's usually not active; she knows it's there on her neck, and she's thereby never too distracted by ephemera while we're on a walk or hunting. But sometimes it is active, and sometimes I use it, though on the lowest setting, which is just a vibration, really. I consider it a reminder that she is not alone. And anything that will regulate a dog without physically hurting it, or hurting its true nature, is okay by me.

Is an e-collar really any different than a check cord or a spike collar? No. You can remind your dog to heel by pulling on a leash or check cord, or you can capture its attention with a slight electronic vibration. I now believe, and have supporting evidence from many pointing-breed owners, that an e-collar is a valuable training tool. Although years ago the collars were one-level shock-inducing horrors, today they are as humane as a choke collar—when used properly as a training tool and not an instrument of punishment. But although I use one now, I'm still glad that before Reilly was a year old, she never had an e-collar on her neck.

So I kept on with John, starting each morning by eight. As we walked the dogs, Tully, Tabasco, Bo, Reilly, and Britta, I told John about Spearfish, South Dakota, and how we should drive there and hunt, just us and our dogs.

"Reilly, I gotta tell ya, is a few years off from that," John said, the tell-it-like-it-is trainer, and not the hunting friend, informing the conversation. "Now, if you want to go out there with Bo—we can see about that."

"Have trailer, will travel," I told him. I watched the block-bodied Bo, as stocky as male German shorthairs get, nearly rottweiler-size, brown and bullish and big-headed like a chocolate Lab, weave in and out of pines and hardwoods, and I thought of how cool it would be to see his stocky body ripping through cornfields in search of South Dakota pheasants. Just then, Reilly began to yip like a coyote pup. She was up a rise at the head of the next trail, waiting for everyone to catch up, her tongue out, her head shivering, all nervous energy waiting for release in the orchard. *Waiting for birds.*

CHAPTER 8

Obedience Training and the Power of the Point

IT TRULY IS A MAGNIFICENT DAY WHEN AN OBJECT OF YOUR LOVE achieves what you, the lover, believe to be a level of greatness. Reilly on point was a picture of style—tail cocked straight, with a slight kink a couple inches below the tip, leg and shoulder muscles ripped from training and rippling with definition, chest out and head up, top lip curled under to expose one side of her canines, and floppy ears cocked so that you might see the 07 tattoo on her right ear. After stroking up her tail at the now infrequent times when she wasn't lifting it on her own accord, John Offerman had to constantly unflip her earflaps as she pointed—an amusing and lasting image.

Seeing Reilly point birds was a dream for me. She was about one week shy of her first birthday and was pointing rock steady on released quail, showing no fear of a gun (John had traded the starter's pistol, which actually was now lost in the orchard somewhere after it had fallen out of his jeans pocket, for a 20-gauge shotgun). She was holding six out of ten points steady to wing and shot. John still had to pin her down with the check cord on those four out of ten breaks, but when he released her after a successful point, she began to visually track the bird till it disappeared in a hedgerow or off into the woods—a success of Reilly's genetics. And she would meander back to us, though not in a rocket-straight line, when called. John told me she was hunting her way back to us, which was a good sign of a spirited dog, though he was still a bit wary of her loosey-goosey obedience.

He had been working with her on the "come 'round" command, and "heeling" and "whoaing" her around the kennel yard. And on our morning walks, we whistled all the dogs back to us, the older dogs, the setters, setting a good example of obedience for Reilly.

Her obedience was coming along; she was responding to "whoa" and "come 'round" and had no trouble with "free" and "get on" as she was let out of the starting blocks. She had outgrown all of her puppiness and was a late adolescent, and a pretty little lady at that. She had grown up fast. In horse lingo, she was about three or four hands high, weighing about thirty-five pounds, much more defined from the side than from the front, from which view she was skinny as a rail.

I was just back from my last trip of the summer, to California where we visited my sister in Los Gatos and C's parents in the Bay Area. From there we continued south to the central coast and happened upon the cute oceanside village of Avila Beach, just outside San Luis Obispo. Sitting on the beach one afternoon, we decided that we would move to Avila if we ever had the chance. We decided we'd shoot for the spring of 2001, after C finished her master's degree. This became a guiding life plan over the next six months.

During a morning walk in late August, I told John about our impending plan of moving to central California in three months, six months, eight months? He had lived in the Los Angeles area for a time, he told me.

"There's nothing for you there," he said. "There's nothing there for guys like us. Dog guys—hunters. There are fewer hunters all the time." Chet had told him long ago, John confided in me, that this tradition of bird-dog breeding and training and hunting over dogs was dying out. He recruited John, just as he had recruited Brendan

Banahan, to have some young bucks still around after he was gone to carry on these traditions of running bird dogs in open fields, of training them to wing and shot in an orchard designed for that purpose, of working with a dog every day to develop a bond that is incomprehensible to anyone who hasn't gone through that process.

John told me, then, a story about his dog Bo. Bo Loves Birds was the actual name of John's shorthair. He got him in Pennsylvania as a newly whelped pup. John was a first-time hunting-dog owner and wanted to train Bo. Then his wife, Karen, faced a tragedy. A parent died. Karen clung to Bo, holding on to the puppy as if he were a soul pacifier. For days, she was consoled by Bo—the puppy smell, the muscular body, the sleepy groan of the dog, the dog's attentive eyes, its need for a scheduled feeding and walk. All completely mundane activities that would avert one's mind from a tragedy and save one from heartache.

"These aren't machines," he told me. "These are family; Riles is your family. You did a good thing by leaving her here. I know you've missed her." We were standing by a little plank bridge over a creek no larger than a ditch; one of the setters sat belly-down in the water. Reilly was nowhere to be seen.

"These are our family," John said. "Reilly needed help. She's good, very good. She has a good home, I see that, and I'm happy. She'll be a good dog." He stopped and whistled. Then he turned to me. "But be patient. Not this year. It'll be a while. But she'll get there."

CHAPTER 9

For the Love of a Hunting Dog

THE GROUSE HOUSE WAS SOUND. I HAD BEAT OUT THE BAD, PUNKY wood within the walls in the corner (one-inch plywood was the core of the walls), replaced it with foam insulation, and reinforced those walls with steel plates. I scrubbed the outside of the trailer, using a barnacle-freeing boat wash, and now the aluminum siding shone as if it were no earlier than 1992, much less 1972, when it was first hung. I had an electric brake box installed in my truck, I refilled the propane tanks on the trailer, I cleaned the plumbing system. I was ready to ride. Where was I going? Nowhere, yet.

September brought John and me to the planning stage of "When will the dog be ready?" All the table training was showing results: Reilly was steady on point, barrel-chested, and stylish with tail and haunches high. Robert Wehle wrote in *Snakefoot* about his comportment standard in a pointer, which I followed as a guide. He described a desirable English pointer as having, among other features, "a large, square muzzle; a definite stop at the eye; a balanced head . . . stomach tight and well-tucked up; hind quarters square and straight with a slight slope to the tail set, with plenty of angulation in the hind legs,

but always square; tail mounted high and carried high; while pointing, tail straight without hook or sickle; gait square and smooth;
markings pleasing to the eye; color deep and rich."

I can't bring myself to parse the behavior or nature or comportment of my dog, vis-à-vis training or her natural behavior, based on
those physical terms outlined above. Do we need such terms to define
a hunting dog's value before even learning the dog's nature? Does this
bespeak advocating a master race of dogs? Bob Wehle was striving for
the ultimate dog within the breed of English pointer; it was his life's
work. He bred great dogs, champion field-trial dogs. Dogs that will
be remembered in the fraternity of dog people for a long time, maybe
for all time. Wehle's books are instructive. You should read them. You
will learn from his methods; you will be entertained by his opinions.

Wehle's *Wing & Shot,* in my opinion, is the best pointer-training
book ever written. I didn't read it till my pointer was three years old.
It is the best primer I've found from which to learn the basics of
training a pointing dog. It is a lasting book that, with foresight from
some publisher, should never be out of print.

All this doesn't change any of my feelings about my dog. Reilly
fits many of Wehle's criteria, but she is not a Wehle dog; she doesn't
need to be. I don't trial her—I hunt her; I live with her; sometimes
she sleeps near my feet on my bed. She does have the hunting stuff,
and that's all I've wanted from her. She has angulation. Half the time,
she has a hook in her tail while pointing, though I'm sure she doesn't
know it. She has liver spots, deep and rich, around her eyes, pleasing
to my eye.

But more than her physical aspect, I've become more and more
endeared by her personality and performance. She has integrity of purpose, and I write that without any intent to judge her based on
human-behavior mores. She has good breeding, good genes, and therefore has a natural hunting-to-point instinct. She is a dog, and I have no
pathetic fallacy to the contrary; she's not my kid, she's my dog. She's a
huge part of my life. How do you define love in your life? You can

love your house, love your car, love your shoes or boots or leather jacket or "Kind of Blue" by Miles Davis. I love my dog.

The training was paying off. And I loved to be around her, watching her learn what she was born to do—hunt and point birds.

I read a book called *Colter* by Rick Bass. I found it on the front counter of a bookstore on Lake Minnetonka. Bass had read there the week before, I guess, and the books were still front and center. I read the book cover to cover in the Minneapolis airport, waiting to fly back to Albany, and was bothered by one passage. In the early chapters, Bass draws a wild conclusion that because his German shorthair, Colter, is judged to be a one-of-a-kind dog by one of the best shorthair breeders in the country, his dog is the best hunting dog in the nation. Why anyone would say that is beyond me. Good breeding is all-important— it's huge. Good training really counts—it's epic. But the best dog?

In July of 2000 I read a review in the *New York Times* of *Colter*, which panned Bass for having a love affair with his male dog. The reviewer, Richard Conniff, identified at the end of the review as someone who was "working on a book about wealth and human behavior," went on to suggest that Bass had an unnatural relationship with his dog. Colter had belly-rubbed a hole in the ground outside the door of Bass's writing studio, where he liked to sleep as Bass tapped away at some of the more important environmental writing of our time. Conniff wrote in the *Times* review:

> The bond between man and dog is at times almost marital. Once, when Colter's away being trained, Bass yearns over the worn patch of ground where his dog normally sleeps: "I have run my hands over the inverted cast of those deep shoulders and bony hips and I lie down in it, to get a dog's-eye view of the world." Another time, he goes hunting with a friend's dog

and leaves Colter back in the pickup truck, his nose pressed against the curve of the windshield. "I feel like I'm being unfaithful," Bass laments.

So Bass was weird, a bona fide freak living in the wilds of Montana, just because he loved his male dog, over which he shot birds and hunted among friends? So went the review, as I understood it.

Well, the ending to the book was a downer. Colter was shot by a true Montana freak with a .22; his remains, and evidence of the caliber of the gun used in the shooting (via the size of the entry wound), were found. Bass was without his hunting dog. More from Conniff:

> The burden of being both a hunter and an environmentalist also weighs heavily on [Bass's] mind. And perhaps because his position is too delicate to make light of either side, he misses that essential ingredient of all good hunting and dog tales, which is humor. Or maybe what Bass has is a dry sort of High Country humor we benighted coastal sorts just don't get.

I gave *Colter* to John Offerman because his Bo was a German shorthair, the same as Colter was. John loved it. He read it entirely over the course of a week, he told me. I never got the book back.

CHAPTER 10

Working on Steady to Wing and Shot

I HAD FINISHED OFF THE TRAILER TO MAKE IT ROAD AND CAMPING READY. The walls were patched and sound, the windows and roof air vents were weatherproofed, the toilet and water lines were cleaned, drained, and flushed. The water tanks were full, the fridge was chilled. The two-inch trailer ball off the back of my pickup, anchored to a heavy-duty undercarriage towing rig, fit the trailer's hitch like hand in glove. The brake lights and turn signals and running lights on the trailer all checked out. The electric brake control was installed under the truck's dashboard. All systems were go. I even practiced backing up with the beast.

C and I took the Grouse House on two test voyages. The first was to Woodford State Park in southern Vermont. A terrible argument ensued during the parking phase. I was sure C was messing with me as I attempted to back into the narrow camping space, backing toward a jackknife, pulling out, backing up again, with the same results each time, none of them good. C kept on with "A little more left; a lot more right" for long enough to frazzle me. After about ten tries and half an hour later, I got the trailer on fairly level ground. The tears in C's eyes when I got out of the cab of my truck (I had yelled a blue streak from the cab of my truck) told me that she had no agenda—she'd been earnest in her attempts to help a bullheaded man park his unwieldy camping craft.

Next we went to a private campground near Tanglewood in Massachusetts, where we saw Tony Bennett and Diana Krall with my parents, who came over for the show from central New York. That Labor Day weekend of 2000 was a washout—it stormed like hell above Tanglewood. Someone was struck by lightning, the rumor circulated. Mom and Dad stayed in the trailer the first night, and C and I were flooded in our tent. The next night, after the show, my parents went to a hotel room. C and I made good use of the back bed in the trailer, with rain beating over our heads. What satisfaction I felt for the weatherproofing work I had done!

In preparation for Reilly's first hunting season, her training intensified for the next two weeks. Every day, she pointed birds in the morning and John worked her on field commands in the afternoon, in preparation for the graduation field test that John and I had agreed on: a released-bird hunt in late September at the farm, with chukar partridge and quail.

On graduation day, John, wearing a faded blue polo shirt and jeans tucked into his rubber boots, planted a couple birds around the orchard grounds. "Reilly knows the quail," he told me, "but wait till she sees the chukar. Shoot when they get up. Shoot quick. But just go ahead and shoot. They get up quick and flare—not like a grouse. We don't want these birds to get away, if we can help it." Better for us to shoot them than to offer them up as fare for coyotes or foxes, was the message.

I knocked down quail on each of Reilly's first three points. Steady. No gain. No creep. Staunch, with a high, rigid tail. A wood-stiff pointer point. She half retrieved these birds, too, picking them up with a soft mouth, but not bringing the birds to hand when called. John said we'd work on that next year. For now, he said, it was important that she was pointing so well and didn't chew up the birds.

"If you want her to retrieve, we'll work on that." I told him that'd be fine, if the training fit the dog's disposition.

Then came the chukar.

Reilly found the first of these birds by a stone wall, but it flared away and John missed with a shot from his 20-gauge. We marked it, and I hitched on Reilly's lead and led her down toward the bird. She pointed it a second time, though not completely stylishly, as the bird was wind-washed and not so full of scent. She crept toward it a bit, or tried to as I held her; her tail was not at full mast. I tried and missed the shot, and that bird flew directly to the pond on the property.

Reilly, against my commands to "whoa," ran down to the pond and established point facing the stone fence at the water's edge. When John and I got there, no bird was in sight. He released the dog, and she leapt at the stone wall, digging at it, whining and barking. Did the bird drown? Or did it burrow into the gaps in the stones? I came forward to "whoa" her. Told her to be easy. John followed, said the bird clearly was under the grass or had taken up residence in the rock wall. We never found it. It never came out.

"Cagey birds," John said. "Just like grouse. You can hit one and it'll disappear."

Reilly was jumpy after that, so we staked her and brought out Tabasco and one of the other setters to find the second chukar, though to no avail. And then graduation was over.

Reilly had done well on the birds. I just wanted to get this year-old doggie back into my life. I said my good-byes to John and called Reilly to the cab of my truck. She jumped into the passenger's seat, panting and drooling. It was as if she hadn't missed a beat from the day back in July when I dropped her off. I told John I'd stay in touch through the hunting season and asked him to let me know how Bo did. Then I gave him a picture of him and Reilly I had taken in the orchard, held in a heavy silver Orvis wing-shooting frame. He was touched. He told me it would go up in his house.

John thanked me and handed me my last invoice for the September training and the birds used in Reilly's training. I told him that I couldn't express my thanks strongly enough for letting me tag along on all those morning walks and training sessions in the orchard. In the subdued way of hunters, we nodded to each other, and I drove off toward home in North Bennington, where C waited to welcome Reilly and me.

It was September 21, and grouse season had already opened that year in Vermont. Reilly had been at the farm for about two and a half months. She smelled of cedar chips and dirt and something dead she had rolled in that week. I was ready to make her my dog again. C said she would give Reilly a bath. And I thought about getting the dog in the woods in search of wild grouse and woodcock.

Chapter 11

Home from the Trainer's

Now what? When I got Reilly home from her summerlong stay at the trainer's farm, at the tender age of one year and one month old, she was natural in her ways around the house—quick to jump on the couch for a nap, never apprehensive to wedge between C and me in the bed, a healthy appetite, and an all-around pleasant puppyish demeanor. In the yard, she was responsive to basic commands such as "whoa" and "come 'round." All seemed, if not fine, at least pretty good. I had my dog back, and she knew who I was; after all, I had spent a couple days a week, most weeks, training her with John Offerman. And she remembered our house, by all evidence, knowing exactly where her dog dishes were and the bedroom and her favorite sunny nook on the floorboards near the daybed in the living room.

But all this nesting turned around when I let her loose in the woods behind my house. I had the run of about ten wooded acres owned by my landlord over the creek off the grassy field behind the house; that was abutted by another forty or more acres still undeveloped and unposted and open for hunting.

On her second day home, I took Reilly back to those woods, leaving a ten-foot check cord on her as John had suggested. "Keep her slowed down by letting her drag a cord," John said. "It'll tangle her up, even, which will teach her she needs you close by. Just try to get her around wild birds. It'll give her a focus and teach her to hunt with you."

John was earnest in his advice. It sounded like a passable theory. Until I tried it.

I let Reilly loose in the woods, and to say she was unappreciative of the alpha male human in her life during these walks would be an understatement. She wore a bell collar so I could follow her whereabouts—but that was all through sound and not vision. When she hit the woods, it was off to the races. She would range left to right, right to left, often stopping and lifting her head. She would catch the scent of something, and then no command would turn her back toward me.

The first time this happened, as I hoofed through the woods behind my house hollering and blowing the Acme Thunderer whistle I had ordered from Dunn's, I said a silent prayer that I wouldn't hear the screeching of tires and the thump of a thirty-something-pound white dog against a Volvo bumper. After she had her fill of searching and hunting—half an hour later, at least, that first day—she came back to her winded and sweating owner, her check cord covered with clusters of burrs.

I went to the hardware store the next day and bought a twenty-two-foot length of 1-inch-thick braided rope and a brass clasp. I tied the clasp to the rope, using a surgeon's loop, and I hitched the clasp to Reilly's collar. We went to the woods. For that day, the long, thick rope slowed her; she moved tentatively through the trees, aware that she was being held back.

The next day, the rope had no such effect. She ran off, sniffing the ground for as long as I saw her. I followed, cursing; then she was gone in the prickers and slash.

For another half hour or so, or until she tired, I yelled while she explored. There was a road with moderate traffic just below my house. Coyotes and bears and foxes were local threats, as was the neighbor with the .22 if Reilly showed up in his garden patch.

Within four days of having my dog home from a professional trainer, I didn't know what to do about her runaway tendencies. She was beyond my control, in no shape to hunt. Though the bird season wasn't yet open and I wasn't carrying a gun, I was hoping, perhaps against hope, that we would find a wild grouse, and she would revert to style and lock on point. I would come up behind her and flush the bird, and she would stay steady to wing. But of course, this did not happen.

I called my friend Brendan Banahan, and he asked me at what level I'd set the training collar for Reilly, and whether she was responding.

A training collar for Reilly? I answered.

John had told me repeatedly that you don't want to hurt a young dog by using a shock collar. He hadn't with Bo, who's five, he told me, and I shouldn't need to with Reilly. He knew her disposition, head-strong though gentle of nature. He advised instead that I run Reilly before each hunt to tire her out some before she hit the woods.

But Brendan, who had used an electronic collar on his pointer, Nell, looked at it differently: "The big risk is that the impatient owner takes out his frustration with the dog by punishing instead of training the dog to perform in a certain way. Long distance is one of the best uses when we can't be right up there with the dog to teach the desired behavior. I have used the collar very sparingly. Not all dogs are candidates for consistent collar training. Nell was defiant when out of reach and was notorious for long-distance hunting (read: exploring the next county!). I was careful not to use the collar when she was out of view, but sometimes it was the only way to bring her back in. I always tried to have her see me with the controller so she understood that the reprimand was coming directly from me. Early on, she recognized the collar and became very submissive as soon as I took it out of the box. Her behavior improved immediately with the collar. Minutes after I took the collar off, she was back to her old habits. This is a common problem with field-trial dogs that are being shortened up to be shooting dogs."

Reilly was from field-trial stock. She was showing signs of block-headedness. She was long-distance running. Seeking reassurance of some sort, I asked Brendan to explain further what he had done with Nell.

"The collar was helpful to a certain extent," he said, "but you can't shock genetics. I also think the collar is a great tool for breaking bad habits, but you need to know your dog and be very selective in deciding which habits need the collar. Using the collar to break a dog of chewing birds could be a mistake. Associating a shock with retrieving a bird could be disastrous. Chet [Cummings, who trained Nell] also recommended strongly against using the collar to keep a dog from breaking. Dogs learn by rote and by experience, but when discipline is necessary, be selective and know what works best for your dog. The newer collars of the last few years with the built-in warning device provide a gentler reminder before hitting the meltdown button. I'm sure that many dogs with real potential have been harmed by the impatient trainer trying to shock compliance into a dog as a substitute for patient training."

I studied the Dunn's catalog. I called another friend and dog owner with whom I had hunted, Jerry Gibbs, the fishing editor of *Outdoor Life* magazine. Jerry's Brittany, Spirit, was a mature male, an obedient and hardworking dog. Jerry told me there was really no way around the collar—you just had to be very careful not to misuse it or, as Brendan said, overuse and abuse it.

The next day, I ordered an Innotek Free Spirit, an inexpensive model with a transmitter range of only about five hundred yards; other more technologically advanced though pricey models have ranges surpassing a mile. It arrived by two-day delivery. I couldn't see paying more than $200 for a training collar, and I told myself I wouldn't need to have it on Reilly much anyway. When it came, I was reluctant to use it, based on John's advice not to. I also felt a certain level of betrayal, that all John had worked for with Reilly might be injured or erased through the introduction of an electronic collar.

I reread the one page in *Pointing Dogs* where Roebuck gives his feelings on electronic training aids: "It would appear to me, I regret to say, that we have now entered an era in which many trainers, professional as well as amateur, appear to think that these devices are essential. And I for one think it is a pretty sad state of affairs." I fell into a deeper funk of conscience.

I reflected on the past week of runaway days. Was Reilly willfully bolting to get back at me for leaving her in a kennel for those months? Dogs are not that clever—or vengeful—I told myself. I thought of the unrestrained morning walks at John's. Of course, she was used to bolting, charging off on her own. She checked back to see where we were, and she never ran off out of earshot, but she certainly had a good degree of independence.

"There are no shortcuts to training a dog well and certainly the use of electronic devices by an inexperienced trainer, who is, after all, learning himself, should not be considered," Roebuck writes. Heady words for me to read, at the time. Still, something had to be done.

I took Reilly out to the woods behind my house, up a trail, and released her so that she could drag the twenty-foot check cord. In an instant, she was gone in the heavily leafed woods. I pursued and called for about twenty minutes. I had put on her bell, but I couldn't hear it. I whistled and yelled and went *"Hi-yawwww"* in the deep bellow that John taught me that was supposed to cut through the clutter of the canopy and understory. No dog. I'm all alone in the late-September woods. Birds chirp and then call shrilly; or is that the dog's bell?

My ears are ringing from blowing the whistle; a buck creeps down the game trail above me, stops to test his antlers against a tree, and then bounds away when I lay into the whistle. I'm not far from the road, only about half a mile from my house. Yelling and whistle-blowing and shouting *"Hi-yawww"* as I am, my neighbors must think I'm nuts.

Still agonizing over the question, which I had elevated to moral status, I talked with C about whether to use the collar on Reilly. C was all for it, for safety reasons. Reilly had already run into the road several times, stopping traffic, and she was getting beyond our control out in the field behind the house. She was a headstrong dog—a blockhead, as Brendan called his pointer.

The shock collar was called Free Spirit—Orwellian doublespeak, as the entire point of the device was to regulate, even relegate, a dog's free spirit. I read the directions and watched the video, and then chose the lowest setting on the transmitter as the starting stimulus. The outfit came with a remote handheld trigger mechanism the size of a remote car-alarm switch or the locking-unlocking device for your luxury SUV.

Reilly had trained with a bell and beeper collar at John's, as well as a heavy leather spike collar, so she took readily to wearing the electronic collar from the get-go. Her first time out with it, I still had her drag a check cord. The first touch on the transmitter brought her trotting back to me, seeming unconcerned.

That night, I had Reilly out again in a back field with the collar and long check cord on. Again she bolted. I hit the button to send the low stimulus, but she kept on going. I switched the transmitter's booster switch, raising the stimulus to level three, and hit the activation button as I shouted, "Come 'round." It knocked her off her feet. She sprang up and sniffed around in circles for what hit her. I yelled, "Whoa," and she stayed.

In guilt, I took the collar off Reilly and, holding my fingertips to the collar nodes, hit the low-level button; I felt a mild vibration, like the buzz you felt when you were a kid and you pressed the poles of a nine-volt battery to your tongue. I flipped the booster switch on my transmitter, raising the jolt to level three, and hit the button again with my fingertips still on the nodes. I jumped and yelped at the jolt; it was like touching a live light wire, a sharp tingly zap.

That night, I gave Reilly about twenty treats, a piece of bacon, and some chicken breast. I felt like a sneaky bastard, a coward. Why couldn't I control my dog without the crutch of electronics?

The idea that I was using a crutch wore off quickly, in a matter of days, in fact. Reilly learned what the collar was within that span of time, coming to hand quite gingerly when I was offering to fit the collar on her. To get her attention and get her to respond to my command to check back, the main reason I felt she needed the collar, I activated it maybe once a yard-training session in those first few days, always backed up with the command "come 'round." She would turn and head back toward me, but not come completely to me. She would find something to sniff on the way, and I didn't want to discourage her from hunting independently, so I did not discipline her for that meandering.

When the season began and we were hunting for real, she slipped away from sight, and I called but didn't hit the button for the collar. As if she knew I would not hit her that time or she was out of range, she was soon out of earshot. I called and whistled for at least forty minutes. I scolded her and cajoled. Yes, I hit the transmitter button several times, thinking the shock might remind her that she was supposed to be hunting with me. She was dragging her long, heavy check cord, but a new wave of frustration came over me when I realized that she might be tangled up somewhere where I couldn't hear her yelp or hear the bell tinkle. I walked up a ridge that, with dark approaching, I did not want to walk up.

And then I heard the bell. I sounded a *"Waayyyy-yupppp"* and then blew the Thunderer whistle. I saw her white body coming up the ridge. There, against her front flank, hung the tattered end of the now one-foot piece of rope that used to be her check cord. She had chewed through the rope to get to me.

I worried about her much less after that.

An English pointer at fourteen weeks—with liver spots around her eyes and a white body faintly ticked, Reilly has classic pointer markings. What a joy to have a puppy that will be, as she matures and benefits from training, your companion in the grouse woods.

With only remedial lawn training at six months old, Reilly shows the value of good breeding in this stylish pose. With training, she'll learn to establish point with style.

Pointers, like many spirited dogs, can become destructive when bored. Reilly ate into her dog bed when left alone—and ended up wearing it as a dress.

Reilly hits eight months old. At this time, the author exercised her as much as possible to wear off her puppy pudge.

Trainer John Offerman did not believe in using electronic collars; instead, he used a spiked training collar to restrain or correct Reilly.

The quail pen in John Offerman's training orchard. John would flap his ball cap in the pen to send a bird toward the hatch so he could capture the bird and plant it in the field. Exposing a dog to live birds is one of the major advantages of professional training.

John Offerman works Tabasco, a setter who was being trained at his kennel at the same time Reilly was.

Reilly goes on point, but John Offerman keeps the check cord in hand, not wanting to risk her breaking and pouncing on the bird. This is the beginning of steady-to-wing-and-shot training.

Reilly points a planted quail, and John Offerman readies to keep her from breaking by pulling on the check cord, if he has to. She becomes more staunch on point as John observes.

A successful pointing sequence: Holding the check cord, John Offerman whoas Reilly, walks in to stroke up her tail, and then in a low voice tells her to be easy. These are the building blocks of steady-to-wing training.

John Hayes of Kirby Mountain Kennels in Vermont's Northeast Kingdom reintroduces Reilly to field training after she was away from professional training for eight months and became spoiled by the author during a winter as a house dog. "If I let her off this check cord, she'd be off to the next county," John said at the time.

John Hayes demonstrates how solid training yields solid pointing-dog results. Even with the author circling his dog and snapping photos, Reilly doesn't break point. Through weeks of repetition, John accomplishes this without the use of a check cord or an electronic collar.

John Hayes holds Saturday seminars for clients who have dogs at his kennels in Vermont. You're invited to come, watch, listen, and learn. Seeing a dog like this Brittany on point drives home the value of professional pointer training.

John Hayes with the tools of his trade: an electronic collar transmitter and a whistle.

The author steadies Reilly on point in one of their favorite Northeast Kingdom coverts.

PHOTO BY TERRY GIBSON

PHOTO BY TERRY GIBSON

The point of the entire training exercise: dog and owner on a walk in the woods.

PHOTO BY ROBIN MIGDELANY

CHAPTER 12

Have Travel Trailer, Will Travel—
Out into New Coverts

TWO WEEKS INTO THE 2000 BIRD SEASON, REILLY HAD NOT YET POINTED
a bird. I had heard a couple of grouse flush wild upon her advance,
but these were only close encounters and not hunterly dog-to-bird
contacts. I had made a pact that I wouldn't shoot at wild-flushing
birds—a pact that was ridiculously easy to keep, since I hadn't had a
clear flush to tempt me.

Still, I wasn't worried. Reilly was hunting closer than two weeks
before. My feeling was that she was becoming reacquainted with me
as the alpha male, as the memory of John Offerman as the guy who
fed her and loved her up for the past few months faded from her
memory. She was keying more on me—and I hadn't found any reason
to be tempted to abuse the power of the training collar. It was time to
hit the open road in the, well, Open Road.

The plan was to drive to Newport, Vermont, far north in the
state's Northeast Kingdom, on Friday, October 13, in my refurbished
1972 Open Road travel trailer, the Grouse House. My friend and editor colleague, Phil Monahan, was to ride shotgun as we towed the
trailer up to hunt with Jerry Gibbs.

This was to be a reunion. Phil and I had made a trip to Jerry's two years before. We'd spent the night at Jerry's house and started off the evening with a couple tumblers of Bombay Sapphire martinis with Jerry and his longtime friend and dog owner and trainer, Lee Leone. After dinner, Jerry, Phil, and I sat in Jerry's living room drinking more clear fluids and talking about magazine publishing. Phil had worked at *Outdoor Life* in the late 1990s; I was there in the early 1990s; Jerry had been with the magazine forever, taking over as fishing editor in the 1970s after the great Joe Brooks.

Jerry and Phil were off getting ready for bed. I sat before the fire, waiting for a bathroom to open up, nursing a cigar, and speaking in a low voice to Jerry's dog, Spirit. The teenage Brittany was acting up a bit, growling from time to time. As I reached down to rub his belly, he leapt to his feet and bared his teeth, warning me with a throaty groan. I reached toward his muzzle, starting to say, "You know me, boy . . . " but before I could finish with "we're all gonna hunt tomorrow," he had clamped down on my thumb. I jerked back my hand and ripped open the plump flesh against the outer thumbnail, clear down to the bone.

Thankfully, Phil was sober enough to drive me to the emergency room in Newport, and I was patched up enough to hunt over a happy-go-lucky Spirit the next day. I even coshot with Phil a grouse that Spirit pointed; he and I shot at the same instant when the bird flushed, so we shared credit.

Needless to say, with all that fun and excitement under our belts, the three of us looked forward to a rendezvous. This time Reilly would hunt in place of Spirit, who was past his hunting days. (Though Spirit did try very hard to mount the already-spayed Reilly at any open opportunity—an act that seemed to delight Jerry and indicate that his wonderful pointing dog was not that geriatric after all.)

At just about the last minute in my Columbus Day escape, Phil canceled on me. But I was not giving up. I'd drive the two hundred miles myself up to the northern reaches of the Green Mountain State, about twelve miles from the Canadian border, Reilly in the place formerly reserved for Phil—the shotgun seat. I had made a reservation at a campground on Lake Memphremagog, the gorgeous glacial lake along which the town of Newport sits, and about half of which Vermont shares with the province of Quebec.

Driving from Bennington to Brattleboro on Route 9 was white-knuckle, over thirty-two-hundred-foot Hogback Mountain and down and through the winding passes that followed. The farthest I had taken the trailer before this trip was about twenty-five miles, over to Massachusetts from my house in southern Vermont. Now, going up a mountain road, the trailer rocked and listed. Several times it pushed my truck uneasily on windy descents. I'm sure, at about thirty-six hundred pounds, it was too much of a tow load for my light six-cylinder Toyota Tacoma. I was mindful—hell, I was scared—of reliving a real-life episode I'd faced on an overland journey when I left Brooklyn to work as an editor at a fishing magazine in Minnesota. I fictionalized the account, to a point, in the novel I was writing at the time:

> My small truck shuddered to life as I let out the clutch pedal and the rental trailer groaned and we were on our way toward the Verrazano-Narrows—though not on an expedient path. Commercial traffic was banned from the Belt Parkway, so we detoured through Sunset Park to Bay Ridge; C. C. [my fictional girlfriend] had the directions down, daughter of Brooklyn that she was. We boarded the bridge in Bay Ridge to cross New York Bay above the very mouth of the Hudson River. It was dark. The bright white light of pairs of headlights came toward us over the Narrows above Gravesend Bay; the pulse of brake lights beckoned us across. Now we were happy. We were passing over a barrier that was a bridge and not an impediment. I felt the same excitement I feel any-

time I approach a New York City crossing; only this time, I was bidding the city good-bye.

We bumped onto the bridge, stopped at the toll plaza, paid the toll, laughed and slapped hands. And as C. C. pulled a champagne bottle from her bag and pulled off the foil, we hit a heavy bump. The bump seemed to lift the back of my little truck. The cork popped. I said, "What the shit was that?" She said, "Nothing but the cork." I said, "Something is not right." She said, joking, "Oh, shut up and drive." That's when we felt the shimmy, the shudder, and the slam.

The double-axle rental trailer, with all my earthly possessions packed in it, was much too much of a payload for my wee two-wheel-drive, four-cylinder Toyota, and it pulled the hitch ball clear off my back bumper. The loosened trailer stayed attached to me only by the safety chains, though it bumped the back of the truck several times as we were accelerating to about sixty miles per hour. My girlfriend and I were not killed. My truck or the trailer didn't tip. The worst was that we were stranded in Staten Island, on Richmond Avenue, for the night. The wrecker dropped us in front of a Korean deli, so at least we had coffee and fruit first thing the next morning, after spending the night in the cab of my pickup.

I thought of this, of course, as I plowed down Route 9 toward Brattleboro—aware also of the inauspicious date, on which bad is expected to happen—but relaxed when I got to Interstate 91. Reilly was getting in tune with my emotions and signals, so she was wigged out with me on Route 9, panting and sputtering slobber on the windshield, which did not help with the stress. Once we got to the highway, she curled up in a ball in the front seat and went to sleep.

We got to Prouty Beach Campground on Lake Memphremagog in Vermont's Northeast Kingdom around eight o'clock. I unhitched the trailer, hooked up the power and water, and then relaxed with a Jamesons and Steinbeck's *Grapes of Wrath*. The lights of Newport shone on the lake as I lowered the book to my chest and fell off to sleep, awakened a few minutes later by Reilly yelping through a bad dream. I shook her awake, shut off the lights, put on the fan for ambient sound, and let her curl up at my feet, telling her that tomorrow would be her big day.

There, with the lights of Newport reflecting on the placid water, and the lights of Quebec, Canada, twinkling in the distance, Reilly and I slept together, resting up for our first distant mission hunting from the Grouse House. "Well, dog," I said, "maybe I'll even cook us some breakfast in the morning."

October 14, we awoke to sun on the lake's shore, Reilly and me, seeing first in the distance the spire of the Catholic church on the hill above Newport. That night, a heavy wind had shook free the red leaves from the maples ringing the lake; now browns and yellows were the primary colors. Fine, I thought; fewer leaves mean easier shooting.

I skipped a propane-fired breakfast and hurried instead to meet Jerry as he was dropping off fishing gear for an auction in Derby, and then we went together to the house he and his wife had built in the hills above Newport at the bend in Gibbs Road. Jerry had cut this unpaved logging-style road up the hill when he and his wife, Judy, decided more than twenty years earlier to move out of New Jersey and raise their two boys in the wilderness that northern Vermont was at that time. Nowadays, you might think about going to Wyoming or Montana or even Canada if you want to declare your independence from current culture; in the 1970s, Vermont was that place. And though forgotten by much of the country as a point on the map close to eastern cities yet still largely undeveloped—particularly in the north, where I live—it remains an escape for many, to this day.

I know several people in my area of the Northeast Kingdom who remain off the grid—they have power only from a generator or solar panels, and not from power lines. Sewers? Not within twenty miles of my house. Cable TV? Not even close. I have a well for water, a septic system for waste, and a wood-burning stove for most of my heat. I live in a thousand-square-foot cottage that is easily heated by the wood-stove. I write in a studio outbuilding, in which I also have a wood-stove that does no good in January when, as it did last year, the thermometer—no wind chill included—reads forty below zero. For the record, my computer in the studio did not explode, the lightbulbs in the ceiling sockets did not burst. It was just really cold.

Jerry and Judy moved to Vermont in 1978. "As soon as I got the job with *Outdoor Life,* the first thing I wanted to do was get out of commutersville," he told me. Jerry had worked in New York for magazines, including the men's magazine *True.* He also had taken up an interest in free-diving and was looking for a place where he could literally immerse himself in his hobby—Lake Memphremagog. He and Judy were free spirits who yearned for a sense of place that was all their own. "We looked at the Rocky Mountain West, but the ocean was too far away. And southern Vermont was too crowded. One New Year's Eve, Judy and I and the boys parked in a motel in Derby [northern Vermont], and it looked like a scene in *Doctor Zhivago.*"

Jerry hit it off with the local game wardens he met, who told him about the fishing spots to know—just what he needed for purposes of magazine work experimentation. "The folks in the area were good," Jerry says. "Land was a hell of a lot cheaper here than it was in New Jersey or New York or southern Vermont. We were young, innocent, and crazy at the time. There was nothing up there at the top of the hill at all."

They moved north with no house, only the prospect of owning some land and building. "We bit the bullet through it all. We were camped on this land—we were tent camping on it—and we didn't have a bank loan. We were trying to stay up there as long as possible, and then we had to commute back to New Jersey. Basically, I have memories of going to a meeting with the bank, and we cleaned up pretty well—here comes Judy coming from the tent in a dress!"

They got their house built and stayed for twenty-four years. Jerry and Judy now live near the coast of Maine. When I came up to

Newport with Reilly, they were packing in preparation of moving to the coast before the snow started. In fact, I had met Jerry on the morning of October 14 at the auction house in Derby after he had dropped off the veritable tackle shop's worth of fishing equipment he'd accumulated in his more than twenty years as a fishing writer.

When Jerry told me the year before that they wanted to sell, by way of a wing-nut suggestion, I mentioned that he should try to have the house featured in the house-for-sale section of *Yankee* magazine. Jerry gave it a shot, the magazine featured their house, and it so happened that Jerry and Judy wound up selling the Newport house to a couple from Texas. When I hunted there in the fall of 2003, the house was vacant and a For Sale sign was planted at the base of the drive. The impact of a Vermont winter cannot be prepared for, can only be lived through, and there's no guarantee you'll want to live through one twice—and I say that having lived through ten so far.

The dogs Jerry had through the years were a Lab, a German shorthair, and his best-friend Brittany, Spirit, who died of natural causes in June 2003. "God, I miss him," Jerry says.

Jerry never used a professional trainer for his dogs—there wasn't one in the northern Vermont area back in the 1970s, and he wasn't going to give up Spirit to anyone anyway. He learned from Lee Leone, who has raised and trained many fine pointers through the decades, and followed the advice of as many books as he could find. He was happy with the results. Spirit worked hard for him. He was a memorable dog.

On my visit that year of my trailer migration, Jerry and I walked from his driveway to his bird coverts. I had the e-collar on Reilly but did not turn it on and did not plan to use it. I had her drag the heavy twenty-foot check cord that day, and I dipped and fended off branches as I followed her through the tag-alder woodcock covert in which we started the hunt. She flushed a couple birds wild and pointed two that we didn't hit. A third point resulted in a shot for Jerry, which he missed—it was a tough tower shot—but I marked the bird when it landed. I called Reilly around, heeled her, and we walked to the bird. I saw it in the grass and Reilly smelled it. She pointed. I asked Jerry to walk in, but he told me to go ahead. I did, flushed the bird, and shot it. Reilly ran to it, grabbed it, and brought it between me and Jerry. When I got to her, she gave it up. The bird was not chewed. A success on all levels.

We continued into the deep stuff of Jerry's coverts, into the large alders and pines. Snow blew around that morning, but the day, as often happens in northern Vermont in October, became sunny and warm, with heavy gray clouds clutching Jay Peak in the distance from our view in this covert—which I now call Gibby Covert and in which I hunt with Reilly each bird season.

What a view from this covert! And the birds! Through the years, I've shot my limit of woodcock several times there over Reilly and have had the best numbers of grouse flushes in my life. In 2001, when my friend Ed Scheff, editor of ESPNOutdoors.com and former colleague at *Outdoor Life,* visited northern Vermont, he shot in that covert the largest snowshoe rabbit I've ever seen. We later ate the fried medallions of its meat, and to this day I tie Haystack flies with the hair from that rabbit's feet.

We broke for lunch back at Jerry's and returned deeper back into his coverts in the afternoon, looking for grouse. And then the fun truly began. I'll tell it in real time:

In a thick pine stand, Reilly points a bird, and when Jerry walks in, four birds flush. Jerry, astounded that so many grouse came out of a pine stand, doesn't shoot. I mark one bird and we follow it. In about three minutes, Reilly goes on point. I "whoa" her; she breaks, then stops on top of a rounded rock. She is on point. I push her tail fully upward, stroke her head, and walk past her. A grouse goes up. It levels off near the tops of the pines. I shoot. The bird folds and falls. I just shot my first pointed wild grouse over Reilly. I turn toward Jerry, raise my arms (shotgun in my left hand), and shout: "I have a pointing dog!"

I begin to get teary and I turn away; I don't want Jerry to see that. Reilly, released, is running in circles where the bird should be. She finds no bird. I tell her, as John Offerman taught me, to "fetch dead," repeating the command with an urgent tone. I begin to mutter the despairing words of the empty-handed wing shooter: "I know I hit it; I saw it fall. . . ." Jerry walks over and says, ominously, "The grouse around here are bastards. They'll dig in a hole before you can catch them."

As he says that, Reilly tightens her circling search and comes up with the grouse in her jaws. I don't give her a chance to bring the bird to hand, running to her instead. She has pointed, and sort of retrieved, her first wild grouse. I put down my gun.

I ask Jerry to give me a moment. I take the bird from Reilly, all tongue and slobber, and she doesn't resist. I put the bird in the pouch of my vest and rub her ears. I kneel down and say in her right ear, the one tattooed 07 on the inside skin: "You are number one—the best baby ever!"

For the day, we flushed thirteen grouse and eight woodcock; Reilly pointed six of these. We weren't shooting wild-flushing birds, to keep the dog focusing on pointing and not flushing behavior. But still, I had two birds in my pocket.

I had dinner that night at Jerry and Judy's, and Jerry and I shared the camaraderie that comes following a long day hiking through woods. We replayed for Judy the points and flushes, which was sweetened by the intimate knowledge Jerry and Judy shared of the bird coverts mentioned, having hunted them for two decades. Judy, for her part, didn't miss a beat throughout the dinner conversation. She has had countless similar dinners through the years, hosting hunting and fishing friends and acquaintances, and she's naturally charming and gracious.

We called it a night fairly early—a relief, given the track record of tipping back martinis Jerry and I have had through the years—and I headed back to the trailer on the lake. As I carried in my gun and hunting vest, there heavy in the game pocket were Reilly's first grouse and woodcock. I wrapped the birds in waxed paper and put them in the fridge. Then I sat down to rub the dog, clear a couple ticks from her ears, and sip Irish whiskey.

I met Jerry and Judy the next morning at their house for a breakfast of croissants and eggs with oregano and spicy brown mustard, with baked red onion on the side. Jim Harrison has written about the civilized nature of bird hunting—that you needn't be in the woods at the crack of dawn, as you would as a deer hunter, or even earlier, in the dark, if wild turkeys were your game. Bird hunters can sleep in till the heavy dew has burned off much of the understory in the woods, have a hearty breakfast, have a heavy lunch, and walk it off afterward. If you smoke a pipe, you can sit on a stump and puff away, munching a crab apple, without fear of warding off grouse or woodcock, which tend to stay put much of the day unless pressured by the physical presence of something unexpected. Pipe smoke and apple munching are not much of a bird deterrent, the way smells and sounds are with deer.

Our second day out was not as productive as the first. Jerry and I decided to drive to a couple wooded coverts that would hold ruffed grouse, woodcock preferring soft-bottomed areas in which they can pick out earthworms with their long beaks.

I had forgotten Reilly's kennel for the wayback, as we Vermonters call the pickup bed, so she rode up front with me and Jerry, in the extended cab seating. We went to Jerry's Space Coverts, on the grounds of a former space-research center based in northern Vermont. Two trucks bearing New Jersey plates were parked at the covert pull-off—coverts anywhere are not as secret as they once were, to say the least—so we tried a covert up the road with mixed grouse and woodcock features: piney, then wooded, and then tag-aldered and soggy-bottomed.

We didn't flush a bird. Reilly came up empty, too, though she worked hard and hunted close off the leash (it was just too thick for her to drag the cord), ranging nicely in the back-and-forth sweeping motion that's so pleasing to watch.

We drove around through the afternoon, looking for other coverts that had been in Jerry's repertoire through the years but now were not remembered. The land had changed so much—woods now fields, fields now developments—through Troy and Derby and Newport in northern Vermont. We called it an early day. I had enjoyed the day just hearing Jerry's stories.

That night, we had drinks at Al Diem's house in Derby. Brendan Banahan was staying and hunting with Al and had twelve-year-old Nell with him. She looked aged, heavy from water retained from cancer pills that Brendan was giving her. Sitting in Al's living room, we sipped twelve-year-old Scotch and talked the talk of bird hunters. Al was proud of a setter bitch he had; Brendan and I reminisced about hunting over Nell; I bragged a bit about Reilly's first grouse; Jerry told the story about Spirit eating my thumb.

Later, we had dinner together. I toasted Brendan and Nell and Al and Jerry and Spirit and Reilly—good friends and good dogs. Then Reilly and I went back to my trailer on the shores of the beautiful lake in northern Vermont.

The next morning was spitting snow and freezing rain, and Jerry came to the trailer to tell me he wouldn't be hunting that day. Reilly and I left for home. The ride home on I-90 and Route 9 was uneventful, though full of stress, with the trailer in tow through a rainstorm. Thank God my dog was next to me, I kept thinking, for peaceful support.

C was grateful when we got home. She and I ate the grouse and woodcock—the grouse roasted, the woodcock "breastlet" sautéed in tequila and orange juice and garlic powder—with basmati rice and asparagus, and it was good. We cuddled on the couch before a fire in the woodstove and finished our wine, adoring the dog strewn across our laps, her pink-and-brown piggy nose nuzzled into the pit of my elbow.

CHAPTER 13

Late-Fall Hunting with Dad and Reilly

I SHOT A COUPLE WOODCOCK OVER REILLY THAT FALL, IN COVERTS THAT are now gone thanks to the Bennington Bypass cutting over from New York through Austin Hill in southern Vermont, a habitat-killing demolition of the hunting grounds that used to be within walking distance of my house. But I didn't shoot at another grouse in the 2000 season, after Reilly's first solid grouse point during my day hunting with Jerry Gibbs.

Several times I saw Reilly stutter—point, scamper forward, then point again. She bumped running grouse that I heard flush wild in their puttering way, out of sight. But nothing shootable. I was more attuned to handling Reilly than to shooting at birds, though: being pulled along through the open woods as I held her twenty-foot check cord, calling her around when she got too far up a ridge from me— being a neurotic dog owner. I guess I was still thinking I would have a ready-programmed hunting companion after having Reilly with a trainer for a few months. I learned my role in the program now.

The electronic collar didn't factor into our hunting. I had Reilly wear it, but I didn't use it much. After the initial introduction of the collar, which did shorten her up, I used it sparingly. I didn't want in any way to injure or compromise Reilly's enthusiasm for hunting. She was hunting hard and with flair; she was having fun in the woods. I didn't give a damn about shooting birds; I only wanted her development to continue.

I didn't take the trailer anywhere else that year. I sat in it often, parked in the backyard, with a power cord stretching from the garage for lights and the radio. Reilly sat at my feet as I worked on my novel and edited fly-fishing texts.

Nearing November, I talked with my father about going to a shooting preserve I'd heard about in Camden, New York, not far from where I grew up in central New York and where my parents still lived on Oneida Lake. I called ahead and ordered ten birds for release. Dad and I stopped for a bacon-and-eggs breakfast at Flo's Diner on Route 31. We discussed how Reilly had been hunting and what we might expect—the same way we'd go through the game plan for our November deer hunts: who would take a stand where, and who would do the driving. The autumn before, C was at my parents' with me when Dad shot a deer and we butchered it in his garage—a scene that was not to be repeated, I was asked by C. So this year on the hunt Reilly would join me with Dad instead.

When I was a kid, twelve or thirteen, my best friend's family, the Colellas, were breeding golden retrievers, and I begged my parents for a pup after I had helped birth their latest litter. I had pulled a few pups from Honey, and afterward I had spent days helping feed and clean the whelped pups in the basement pen. I don't remember how many were in the litter, but after a few weeks, one pup was left—the runt—and with my childish imploring, I went to work on my parents.

We bought the dog. My father named her Poppa-Bear's Goldi-locks, that little runty fuzzy golden puppy, and it was my job to bird-train her. Up to that day of getting a pup, I had been my dad's flushing boy. We had pheasants in the fields around our house then, in rural central New York in the early 1980s—it was not unusual to see a cock scamper across Shackleton Point Road as the family headed for church on a Sunday morning—and there were wild grouse in the neighboring woods. I was quite deadly at the time on chickadees and red-winged blackbirds and rabbits with my pellet gun but wasn't old enough for gunpowder-powered guns, so the deal was that I would follow Dad through the woods and flush the running birds we came upon.

Dad gave me a couple bird-dog training books, and under the advice of one, I made a retrieving dummy that was an athletic sock stuffed with old underwear. I took Goldie up to the field behind our house and tossed the dummy a couple dozen times, calling, "Fetch." I reported back to Dad that Goldie was not a hunting dog. I think I shot once from a 20-gauge later, to further prove that she wasn't a hunting dog—scared of the gun!—and that was that. Goldie became the neighborhood dog. She was a gentle, socialized golden and our lifetime family dog. My parents, my brother and sister, and I will always miss her.

When Goldie died, my father called me, late one Saturday night, when I was living in Manhattan. I had gotten home late and had a message from Dad on the machine. When I called him back, he told me the news that Goldie had died. He cried. That same night, I had found out that the father of one of my best college friends had died; I cried, too. The next day, I went to a funeral.

In late autumn of Reilly's first hunting season, I wanted to be in the field with my dad, S. Joseph Healy, who had grown up in the foothills of the Adirondacks in Carthage, New York, in a large, fatherless Irish family. My grandfather, so I'm told because I never met him for him to tell me this history himself, lived with his sisters in the away-from-the-family side of a two-family house, and though he was a well-read and educated man, he split his time between the Carthage library and the local bar.

How does it feel not to have a father? I wouldn't know, since I had one since birth. But my father did not. When I was old enough to appreciate the story, Dad told me how he had come home from college and had seen his father in the bar in Carthage, and his dad, my Grandpa Healy, had sent him a beer. When Dad picked it up, Grandpa nodded and raised his glass in a toast, saying nothing but indicating nonverbal approval of what he had heard about Dad's success in college. My grandfather died not too long after that, years before my parents were married or I was born.

My father learned to hunt from his older brothers. "My brother Mike had a dog, a little beagle named George," he told me. "He was a good dog, and a hunter too. We shot partridge and rabbits over him. He had a great nose. There used to be great rabbit and partridge hunting at the ball diamond in Carthage. I think that dog had a little bluetick in it—it actually was a mongrel. The dog slept with Mike; he loved it. My first gun was a pump Savage, from my brother Donnie. Mike had a Berretta, it was a beautiful gun; maybe he won it in a poker game."

Bird hunting, to my dad, was sport. Deer hunting was what you always did in November. He did this all through my childhood, and I aspired to it from the time I was old enough to walk and had watched him and my uncles and my father's friends dress out and butcher deer in our garage. In high school, that desire faded. But only for a time; it never left me.

Now I hunt deer and I hunt birds. And when I sit in the woods each autumn, I reflect on my central New York and Adirondack childhood. I own my father's decades-old red plaid Woolrich hunting clothes—he lives in Florida and no longer hunts—and I wear them, wool-heavy and musty-smelling in the clothes of a man who grew up in the woods passed on to me. There are burrs in the pockets, I swear, that are probably from hunts twenty years before.

Says my Dad: "You were interested in hunting, and we created a bond that way, and you were interested in fishing, too. And when you got older, too. And the camaraderie was there at a young age. And that developed as a bond when you were young." Dad also told me how bird hunting came into our family experience: "When I grew up, if there were birds there, you went about hunting them. You didn't have your dog on a leash; you went across the street and hunted. It stemmed from my family, my brothers. Donnie [Dad's older brother] was a loner; he liked being in the woods by himself. I think Donnie was the one who taught us all."

By the time I was grown, Dad said, "There was no room to hunt birds. The lack of open space, and urban sprawl, brought you to different places to hunt birds. It wouldn't be spontaneous." Those pheasants in the fields along Shackleton Point Road were long gone by the time I got Reilly. So, no, spontaneous hunting near my parents' house was not an option.

But to have Dad see Reilly hunt was a gift I wanted to give.

The shooting preserve was based at a house surrounded by fields back some ways down a dirt road, with a pheasant pen in the front yard. The house was the same as so many neglected houses in rural areas of central New York and much of Vermont: untended yard, worn-out siding, a porch that's a holding place for plastic yard toys, old furniture, and lots of casual junk. The owner introduced himself as we pulled into the driveway. As Dad and I stretched from the hour's drive, a man with the owner saw Reilly and asked if she was an Elhew.

"Damn, she's got the markin's," the guy said. I mentioned the breeder from whom I bought Reilly. They knew him, and the owner's friend grumbled about him raising pointers that don't carry on the best genes in the pool. Reilly's sire, Comanche's Tonto, was mentioned. I said to them, friendly-like, pointing to Reilly, who was happily relieving herself in the owner's weedy yard, "Well, we can look at the outcome, look at the evidence—this is Comanche's outcome." They nodded. It wasn't a big deal. They asked her age, and I said it was her first season, she just passed one.

The man who asked her lineage complimented her, said she looked in great shape. I mentioned that I'd had her with a trainer for the summer, and that she'd shown spunk this year, but we just hadn't been finding wild birds over in Vermont. The released birds would be good exercise for her.

I shot two pheasants and two chukar; Dad missed all his shots but was amazed by the sturdiness with which Reilly pointed. She even pointed a wild grouse in the woods off the sorghum field in which the released birds were planted.

To this day, Dad talks about that afternoon. He talks about Reilly running down a pheasant through a sorghum row and pointing that cock as it sat on the edge of the row. I ran down to the dog. I shot that bird. Reilly picked it up, brought it to my father. I have the tail feathers hanging off my fly-tying shelf as I write this. One day those feathers will make the legs and wing case of a Pheasant-Tail Nymph. One day the bird's breast feathers will make the claws of a crab pattern. One day I may pass on those feathers to my future son, or to a niece. One day I'll bury those feathers with Reilly.

John Offerman told me during one of our morning walks, after we had talked about hunting in South Dakota and Wyoming and the Adirondacks, and I had finished bragging about the rehab I'd done on my trailer—John told me, quite out of the blue, that when the time came that his shorthair, Bo, couldn't make it anymore, he would do what Chet Cummings had done: fold an overdose of pain pills in the dog's food and carry the groggy body to a grave in the woods. I will do that. I will take pheasant and grouse and woodcock feathers with me. I will bury Reilly with the elements of her life.

Late-season 2000 was tough—cold and snowy. I didn't see or hear a bird in three consecutive trips out with Reilly. On November 20, we hunted a regular covert of mine, a ridge covert, and we immediately busted two grouse. Reilly, birdy, took off up the ridge in the lope that tells me she's gone. I hit the button to activate the e-collar, but it was too late. I called her for about half an hour, whistling with the Thunderer and calling with my bellowing call. She didn't come.

It became dark and Reilly was still gone. I went back to the truck for a flashlight. I kept on whistling and calling. Swearing under my breath, I started thinking about the bears and coyotes that would come out after dark. I started thinking about Reilly losing her bearings and ending up on Route 7, the nearest busy road.

After about an hour and a half, I finally heard the bell coming. I trained the flashlight on the white body to which the bell was attached. She was wagging her tail, unperturbed at having been away from me for so long. Trailing off her collar was the frayed stub of her check cord; she had been tangled and chewed through the rope. She had done this shortly after I had brought her home from John Offerman's training kennel, and she did it again about two weeks after this hunting trip. I was getting tired of buying rope! We needed more time with a professional trainer next year.

Her entire first season in the hunting woods, she'd been eager to hunt, possessing that nervous energy so prized by pointer trainers; she'd been tireless in the field. She'd continued to respond well to field commands, though she still broke often at the sniff of game. I was happy with what she'd gained from a trainer—certainly more than a neophyte like me could teach from book knowledge.

By December we'd stopped hunting, although the season in Vermont continues till the end of the year. I'd had Reilly for one year. Lying in bed with C and Reilly on December 2, the day after my birthday, as I read the *New Yorker* and prepared for sleep, I thought about how lucky I was.

CHAPTER 14

Getting Through Winter;
Losing a Friend

IN FEBRUARY 2001, I MET MY BROTHER IN MIAMI AND WE HAD AN over-the-top dinner, at his request, at a trendy South Beach restaurant. Between the delivery of plates from the tasting menu, Tim, not quite two years my senior, told me he would be proposing to his girlfriend as they visited my parents in Islamorada that weekend. I told him that I'd thought about asking my girlfriend the same question. I missed her, C, and I missed her and me nesting together with Reilly.

Tim did ask Kristen to be his wife, and she is today. I was the best man at their wedding the following summer. I never asked C. We faded away.

Faded away? Well, it's true. For a while that winter into spring, we didn't talk about each other staying together or moving to California, as we had the autumn before. We didn't talk much at all.

Winter passed quickly—it was a snowy year and a good one for Vermont ski areas. I took up snowboarding in earnest, used my time away from the office less for my novel and more for riding at Bromley.

When I got home from the mountain one day in March, C told me there was a message on the machine I had to hear. Her eyes were red. I thought first of my grandmother, then my parents.

Something was bad.

I kicked off my snow-covered boots and ran to the answering machine. I hit the play button. It was Brendan on his cell phone. "Joe, sorry, I tried to call you at work but you weren't there today, I guess. But I'm driving back to Connecticut now and was just at the funeral for John Offerman. He died yesterday. He had liver cancer for a while but didn't want to tell or bother anyone. He was a low-key guy, you know. Christ, he was forty-seven. I'm sorry. Call me when you can."

I felt punched in the gut. I sobbed for about an hour. I thought of my talks with John about hunting out west when Reilly was ready. Bo *was* ready. But John was gone.

I hugged Reilly that night, hard, as I sat on the couch in silence. Funny how dogs read our emotions. She sat still with me, without trying to roughhouse or squirm. I sat and stared at the flames through the door of the woodstove. I knew that time passes, and we all have to get on with it.

I gave a talk at a fly-fishing club in Albany that April, and realized that the way I wanted to connect with people through writing was happening in every issue of the fly-fishing magazines. People cared, people read, people devoted or diverted their time to those magazines.

That night, standing up in front of the club members, more than a hundred fly fishers, I realized I was tired of being, willingly, on the outside. I wanted back into the day-to-day editing of the fly-fishing magazines. So I went back to work full-time that April.

I told C. And shortly after that, she finished her master's degree in social work from the University of Albany. That very night, when she received her degree, I was at the computer writing when she came home. I told her I wanted to be alone. I told her I would not move to

California. I slept on the couch that night. The next day, she moved out.

In June, C's brother flew from California to accompany her on the cross-country drive back. They stayed with me that night. We watched a movie and went to bed. C and I slept together one last time, with Reilly between us.

Early the next morning, before first light, I left for the Albany airport to fly to Miami to cover the Golden Fly Tarpon Tournament. C and I kissed good-bye. Before she left for the West Coast, her last act was to take Reilly to the kennel.

I spent the days of the tournament fishing with masterly guides and anglers and the nights thinking of Reilly and C. Good-bye, I thought of C. Can't wait to get home, I thought of Reilly.

CHAPTER 15

Starting a New Chapter in Pointer Training: The Second Year

July 2001, and I was home alone with my dog. My sleek little pointer. Not exactly where I thought I'd be at that stage in my thirty-something years—coming off a broken live-in relationship with the woman with whom I had brought the dog into the family, and with whom six months earlier I had been planning a life change to the West Coast. No, the joint move, the partnership, didn't happen. And getting the dog was my idea, my task, my undertaking. And her training was still a work in progress.

"So often new dog owners have no planned program for their dog, and just blunder along aimlessly without an organized pattern." So wrote Bob Wehle in his book *Wing & Shot*. I felt myself to be, still, a new dog owner. With John Offerman dead, I was adrift with my own plans for dog training. That first summer, in 2000, with a dog trainer had taught me the value of working with a professional trainer; I knew the best for the dog would be to do so again.

So that July, I suppose I was okay. A touch sentimental, but overall happy. The summer was sunny, and I was doing quite a bit of fly fishing. The magazines I was overseeing were doing well. I didn't have the time, however, for Reilly's field training that second summer, now that I was back full-time at my editorial job. I didn't have the prospect of birds to release—and exposure to birds was arguably the most important element of pointer-dog training, as I had seen through my tutorial the summer before with John. So I'd been trying to find another trainer.

I did a Web search but found no connections in Vermont. I greatly respected the writing of hunting-dog columnist George Hickox of New Hampshire in *Shooting Sportsman* and thought of seeing if he had room in his kennels, but learned that Hickox wasn't doing much in the way of full-time training then. Then I thought of Ralph Stewart.

I had worked with Ralph at *Outdoor Life* in Manhattan in the 1990s. He was now the editor of *Shooting Sportsman,* based up in Camden, Maine. One year, Ralph and I had traveled together from New York to the Northeast Kingdom of Vermont to hunt birds with friends. Ralph, a straitlaced and buttoned-up guy, and I had a ball talking about writing and editing as we headed up Route 91 in his old truck. I haven't hunted birds with Ralph since that time, but all of us who were editors at *Outdoor Life* during that period will always be friends. I asked Ralph if he had any leads on pointer trainers in Vermont.

Ralph suggested that I contact Tim Leary, another writer friend with whom I'd worked on stories for the fishing magazines. Tim recommended a friend of his who owned Kirby Mountain Kennels in Kirby, Vermont. John Hayes had trained a number of dogs from the Manchester area of Vermont, as well as other parts of New England. "He's really good with dogs," said Tim, "and I think you'd like his operation. He does take dogs in for training, usually by the month, and has quite an extensive setup for the pointing dogs in particular."

Tim told me he was taking his setter over to John's on a day-by-day basis. He invited me to call if I came north. I had never been to Kirby; I only knew it as an exit off I-91 on my way to Newport,

Vermont, to visit Jerry Gibbs. I knew almost nothing about the Northeast Kingdom, except for the weekend many years before when I hunted there with Ralph and my time spent with Jerry.

I called the kennels and talked to John's wife, Wendy. I told her I would soon be heading to the ESPN Great Outdoor Games in the Adirondacks, to teach fly fishing to the audience, and would be happy to come northeast first to meet with her and John and introduce Reilly. If all went well, I would then head west across Lake Champlain to Lake Placid, New York, for the games while Reilly stayed behind.

If John Offerman was a seminarian of dog training—Reilly was the first pointing puppy under his full-time training advisement; he was applying all he had learned from Chet Cummings but was still feeling his way through the process—John Hayes was a practiced theologian who had brought the tablets of dog training down from Kirby Ridge to his farm in his fifteen years of dog training. From the first day I met him, I let him know that I was most interested in bringing out the best of Reilly's genes and traits so that she would be the happiest and most productive hunting dog she could be.

John and Wendy Hayes live on a lovely small-farm-sized spread with a pond and mountain views. John moved to northern Vermont from the Boston area; Wendy grew up in St. Johnsbury. They have two children, a girl and a boy, whom they home-school (Wendy is a teacher), and the family keeps many dogs for companionship. John trains dozens of dogs every year—upward of thirty—and he and Wendy breed pointers and flushers, including waterfowling Labs. They have a self-contained bird-dog compound.

"The first dog I got paid to train was in 1987," John told me. "And I had trained a handful of dogs before that time. I trained three dogs the first year, sixteen the next year, and then forty-five the next year. And then it was forty to sixty for the next ten years. Dogs come for an average of six to eight weeks per stay. A month of training? That's nothing. I equate a month to a semester in college. In four months, you get an associate's degree. You know, most people can't even get a job with an associate's degree. You put eight months of training in, you get your bachelor's degree, you're pretty qualified.

"Dog training is very expensive," he continued. "If you want an accomplished pointing dog, it takes about six months of training, and with the purchase price of the dog, you're talking $3,500 to $5,000. Which, in the scope of buying a four-wheeler or a snowmobile, or even a nice shotgun, is nothing. But it is still a lot of money. And then, how much are you gonna use it? As I tell people with pointers, if you're not gonna hunt twenty days a year, the dog can never, ever, come to its full potential. It takes five hundred grouse encounters for a grouse dog to be made. So if you're doing fifty a year, it takes ten years."

I mentioned that it wasn't an easy thing, committing to a professional trainer. He inferred what I meant. "The money is an important factor. But people say, 'I can't leave my dog for two months. I can't do it.' Guess what—in a short time, it's 'Joe who?'"

John, I learned, is no velvet-glove dog trainer. He goes for results. This is not to say he would be severe with dogs under his watch; he simply knows, and will share with you, that training is training and you can't go into the process halfway. "You have to have a tremendous amount of faith in what the trainer is doing," he said. "My goal, as a companion gun-dog trainer, is to make the dog better than when it came here. If I do that, I'm successful. Now, some I make a tiny bit better, some I make a lot better, some I make a tremendous amount better. That's because of flexibility and time, where the dog was when it came in, breeding, and what the people let me do."

He knows dogs, and he knows their owners from the actions of the dog. "Dogs don't lie," John told me, meaning that he can read quickly in a dog how its owner has handled it up to that point. "Within twenty-four hours, I know the whole story of the dog. Without even saying a word, the dog tells me what it's been like in the last year."

My take is that he saw me as a compassionate dog owner who did not have time to bring Reilly to the finish line with her bird training. He was curious to the point of amusement that she hadn't been trained with an e-collar the summer before. I told him I'd used electronics during the hunting season but mainly just to keep her from running out of my hunting range. He asked if that had helped. "So-so," I told him.

He worked Reilly a bit in the yard and complimented her style. He told me he hadn't trained an English pointer in a while but had worked with them and loved the athleticism and intensity of the breed. My biggest concern, I told him, was that Reilly was from field-trial stock, but since I wasn't a field-trialer myself, I hoped to shorten her range. This he acknowledged with a smile and a knowing, "Ohhh yeahhhh." He was only too familiar with a recreational hunter hoping to train a dog from field-trial bloodlines to hunt close. Most bird hunters yearn for a close-working dog.

When I speak to John to this day, he reflects on the training he did with Reilly and reassures me about my choice of breeds. "You were a very motivated person who researched and bought a Ferrari. And when a Ferrari is right, it takes your breath away. But going into corners and crashing, flipping over, and blowing tires, that's tough. Whereas a lesser dog is never a superstar, and never takes your breath away, but kinda pokes its way through the deal. Well, I'd rather be where you are. I want to be coming around the corner, and all of a sudden the dog's going full bore, and—wham! She's on point. But to do that, the key as a trainer—and I had a plan for your dog from the first day I saw her—you need to give that dog her freedom. You gotta make her be under control, but the push-pull on that dog is so fine. She's a very powerful dog, but she's a very soft dog. By soft, I mean that some dogs' feelings get hurt, and they pout—some dogs are like that, and she's one of them. I was laying the foundation for two or three years from the training, which I think has paid off.

"A lot of novices think you want a grouse dog to stop about twenty-five yards away from the bird and creep up on it: tippy-tippy-stop; tippy-tippy-stop. But that'll scare more grouse, because it simulates a fox or coyote. You want a dog that's going warp nine and all of a sudden—*whoop, boom*—it just slams on point, and the grouse goes, 'What the heck is that?' And the dog is just like a statue. And the grouse is a statue. It's what I call a Mexican standoff, because the first one that moves loses. Now you walk in as the flusher and you push the bird. But the dog that's kinda meandering in, tippy-toeing and stopping, tippy-toeing and stopping, the grouse says, 'That's a fox.' A lot of people don't believe your type of dog can be a grouse dog, but she's the type of dog that wins the field trials. She's just a very classy, hard-moving, powerful dog."

My answer? "She's just so much fun to watch."

That first day, John and his family and I had a nice lunch as we got to know one another. He hadn't known John Offerman or Chet Cummings, but he respected the old-school efforts of training without an e-collar. He said he did use a collar and, in his experience, it brought the consistent results that every dog owner he knew looked for. In other words, John understood the ego of hunting-dog owners wanting to see their dog perform in the expected manner: holding steady without breaking on point or in the duck blind; coming when called; retrieving when told to; not jumping on the kids and neighbors. "The best way for anyone to have total control of his dog 100 percent of the time is to use an e-collar," John said. "Using the e-collar properly will ensure that you will get the results desired. The example I use is, boy, I never thought I'd need air-conditioning in my truck in Vermont. But now that I have it, I don't want to give it up. Or power windows, power steering, any of these devices that we use to make life easier. All this stuff is pretty nifty."

He asked me casually, to get a good background on the dog, what the trainer had worked on the summer before.

"Birds, birds, and more birds was the program," I told him. "We covered the basics: field and obedience commands, keeping steady to wing and shot; mostly we had her on quail every day." John nodded and told me most of his training was done with pigeons, which emitted a strong bird scent and were hardy birds that weren't injured by repeated handling. He noticed me looking at his pheasant pen and told me those were for family use.

I also asked about the young dogs I had seen in what looked like a breeder's kennel. "When I first started doing this, breeding dogs was not part of the plan. I was going to be a boarding kennel and a trainer. But as a beginning trainer, I got the horrible stuff. I got everyone's outcasts. I really killed myself at the beginning," John says. But his breeding has developed a talent pool for training. "We raise setters, Brittanys, Labs. Now we have good raw materials: 80 or 90 percent of the dogs trained here were born here."

He told me he was glad I had brought Reilly in her second year; the first three years are when he wants to work with a dog, he said. "I tell people that there's a three-segment life to the dog. There's one through four, when we say to ourselves, 'Why are we doing this?' Four through eight are the real benefit years. And then eight through twelve are the kinda sad years: They've got the brains, they've got the knowhow, they've got the experience, but they can't go as hard anymore. That's when the heart wants to go but the body can't."

I asked John what would happen during the week, when it was him and the dogs in the training field. "Many people think it takes a bazillion hours to train a dog. I work the dog fifteen to twenty minutes a day, five days a week. That's it. First of all, there's consistency. I have a plan every single day when the dog comes out. We always start where we left off the day before, and we try to build from there. A good trainer will always try to have a gradual incline up. Most owners train their dogs inconsistently; they do a lot of stuff with the dog, and then they let it get away with murder. And this is stressful for the dog.

"So I'm bringing the dog out of the kennel, it's been in there twenty-three and a half hours, it's pumped up, it's like a jack-in-the-box. It comes out and it's being made to do what it has to do, right now. No questions; we don't give any slack at all. People say, 'Oh you need to let the dog run around first.' No, I don't. I'm gonna make that dog do what it has to do. I make her do it then so that when you're hunting, it's gonna be easier. People bring me their dogs and think I can wave a magic wand over them—but it's repetition and consistency that make the difference."

If you can be present at training sessions, John told me, pay attention to all that the trainer does, not only with your dog, but with all the dogs. Dogs all have different mindsets, different amounts of power, different instincts. As situations change, a dog's temperament changes. Observe, ask questions at the appropriate times, and learn. Some things a bird dog is trained, such as keeping steady to wing and shot and force break to retrieving, are not natural behaviors. A good trainer is drawing something out of the dog.

"A good trainer will do that without putting fingerprints on a dog. What I mean by fingerprints is that when the dog is on point, it's not putting its head down or its tail between its legs. You want the dog to be bold and to have good style. A lot of novices put fingerprints on dogs because they make the training sessions too long; they want to do it till they get it right, but there's a point where it's counterproductive."

After lunch, confident that Reilly was in the right place, I left her with John.

I knew my headstrong pointer needed a trainer who would help bring out her natural abilities. I couldn't do it—I didn't have the experience; I didn't have a pigeon or quail pen with which to help her reach her potential level of natural birdy acuity. John told me that I was welcome to visit every weekend and learn with him. It was a huge commitment, he agreed, to give up your year-old dog for an entire summer. But my dog was in good hands, and training would begin again.

So I drove down the lane from John and Wendy's, admiring the beauty of the ridge on which they lived. I continued on to St. Johnsbury to meet my *Fly Tyer* magazine colleague, Dave Klausmeyer, with whom I traveled to Lake Placid to hold fly-fishing instruction at the ESPN Great Outdoors Games.

And I missed my dog.

CHAPTER 16

Lessons on Training
a Pointing Dog

OWNING MY FIRST POINTING DOG LED ME TO PROFESSIONAL TRAINERS. That was my way of learning as much as I could about the process of hunting-dog training, in a true evolutionary environment on pace with the dog's development. Not wanting to screw up the genetic gifts my dog possessed from birth, I put her in the hands of pros. But despite my own fears and frustrations at the thought of training Reilly myself, without the aid of a professional trainer, I didn't have blinders on to the fact that, yeah, you could do this yourself.

What I owe to this book and its readers, therefore, is another point of view—one not grounded in a thesis dependent on professional dog trainers. So I'll share some thoughts from a longtime pointer owner who has trained his own dogs, always. Lee Leone of Derby, Vermont, has hunted over pointing breeds for more than twenty-five years. An anesthetist trained in the navy and at the University of Pennsylvania, Lee is a serious man with a romantic nature—a born pointing-breed owner. He has a friendly pedagogical approach to sharing ideas about what he knows well, though he's not a pedant. Lee is a perfectionist, but he knows what he doesn't know. He's proved this to me through his thirst for saltwater fly-fishing know-how, which, through the years, has led him to ask any question that comes to his curious mind without the normal hesitancy of guarding one's lack of experience. He's picked my brain about tarpon flies and leaders and bonefish presentations and the fine points of the double haul; he wants to know, he asks. About dogs, I ask the same of Lee.

Lee Leone is in his early sixties, white-haired and white-mustachioed and fit, and claims to be semiretired. He has three dogs, two setters and a Brittany, which he's trained from puppyhood and houses in a heated kennel in his backyard. Working in the "real world," as we say, Lee is in demand as a freelance anesthetist around New England; he chooses and negotiates the terms of his contracts at various hospitals around the region, which provides a very important outcome: Lee has taken off every fall for the past seventeen years to hunt grouse and woodcock with his dogs. He's also hunted western birds the past couple years. I don't mean just a week or two in the woods; all fall, from September to New Year's, he's out with his dogs. He won't tell me how many days he hunts birds each year, but I'll bet it's at least, as a low-ball estimate, sixty days in the field. He's a hero to me. I truly mean that. Part of life must be to devote time to that which makes you who you are. Lee does that.

Lee also has a superb wine cellar; owns fine guns and nostalgic sporting art; loves good food; has a tremendous and instructive and emulous relationship with his wife, Roz; has raised two sons; and is fun to be around, because he has the life gift of transmitting energy to you in any conversation. The guy's a Boston Italian; that might explain something about his personality. He often makes a point by waiting for your response and then snapping his fingers into a handgun pose and saying, "That's right, that's right. You got it, lad."

He will also make an animated yet cogent case for this or that, and conclude (but never concede) with "You might find somebody who'll disagree with that, but that's my opinion." You just don't meet guys like Lee often enough.

I asked Lee why he chooses to train his own dogs, particularly since he's gone much of the week on freelance jobs that take him from home and Roz and his dogs. Why hadn't he ever sought the help of a trainer?

"Bird-dog training is not a very difficult thing to do. I'm not slamming professional trainers; overall, they have a place, a very strong, solid place. What the professional trainer has that the average person does not have is time, equipment, and the space to use them constructively. Another thing he has is experience. And that experience gives him the capacity to read a dog—he knows when to go forward and when to stop.

"But it's always been very important to me to work with my own dogs because I believe that the trainer imparts his own imprint on the dog. And I like to hunt birds in a certain way, and I like my dogs to handle a certain way. Therefore, I want my dogs to be my dogs; I don't want them trained by anyone else. I want to know every step of their progress. I want to initiate and supervise that so I know where they are at all times in terms of their development. If I have all of that information, I can discipline them appropriately if they need to be disciplined, or I can back off."

"Tailored to the nature of the dog?" I said.

"Exactly!" He snapped his fingers. "I know the dog's personality. And the dog knows me, which is just as important as me knowing the dog."

"How did you start?" I asked Lee. "One of the things I found completely daunting was that I didn't want to screw up Reilly's training."

"I think everybody feels that way. I felt that way too. I was very lucky in that when we moved to Maine when I finished my anesthetist training, the Maine bird-dog club had been formed, oh, a handful of years before; this was in 1971. It was a statewide dog club, and it was sanctioned by the American Field. So their field trials were written up. And there were a lot of great people. Bob Paucek, who's famous in the Northeast and is retired now, and Dave Pierce." One of Lee's dogs is an English setter bitch, Holly, out of Paucek's Tommyknocker, a Grand National Grouse Championship winner.

"There was a very senior member of that group, by the name of Cliff Hale. He was an elderly man and a professional dog trainer and breeder, and that's all he ever did his whole life. I was very young at the time—I'm going back thirty years—and he was well up into his sixties or seventies. He took me under his wing and gave me information on dog training that was so helpful. I was very, very lucky, because for some strange reason, he liked me, he took a liking to this kid. I had a Brittany at the time, and Cliff was an English pointer man—that's all he bred, that's all he handled. And he kept saying to me, 'What the hell are you doing with that dog that doesn't have a tail? When you gonna get a real bird dog?' He liked to tease me. But he was a great guy."

"How did he help you?" I asked. "What did that entail, being taken under the pointer-training wing?"

"Basically, he gave me a lot of advice. I mean just commonsense stuff that sometimes you tend to overlook because there's a level of anxiety, like you've said, about training a dog—you know, *'I'm gonna train a bird dog!?'* That kinda deal. *'Gee. What do I do? Am I doing it right?'* That kinda thing. *'Should I do this more, or should I do it less?'* Basically, what he said to me was, 'Be fair, be firm, and be consistent.' If jumping up on the sofa is bad today, it should be wrong for the rest of the dog's life. Don't give a dog a double message. Commonsense stuff—but sometimes you're so close to it, you just can't see it. And the other thing he said was that the most important command you ever give to a pointing dog is 'whoa.' That dog has to understand what that means, that's all there is to it. You say, 'Whoa,' and the dog stays there till you tell it to move."

Lee mentions that you have to give a dog some latitude if it relocates after a point. For example, Lee doesn't use the command "whoa" with his seven-year-old setter Holly because he lets her relocate after pointing a bird. She points, the bird runs, and she breaks point in an attempt to find enough scent to establish point again. You don't fault a dog for that work.

Early on, Lee says, he used several training manuals. "When I first started out, I had eight, twelve books. My advice to anyone starting out is to get one book, and one book only. But the more you train, the more you like to read about how it's done by other people. Then you're broadening your expertise. Trainers tend to do what works best for them. Some trainers are better at training dogs to be really steady to wing and shot; others are superior at force-breaking to retrieve. These books are chock-full of information, little tips, that the trainers have garnered through years of experience and are passing along. You can assimilate these things into your own training."

I asked Lee if he had any recommendations for selecting a bird dog. "Just because a dog has a sound genetic background for hunting," he said, "it doesn't mean that every dog out of that particular litter is gonna be a great bird dog. And females are not necessarily better than males; they're just more biddable, which means they're easier to train. Neutering does not make a better bird dog, either, in my opinion."

When Lee first brings a puppy home, he keeps it in a travel kennel in the basement of his house. He believes that crate-training is essential to establishing boundaries and control with a young dog. "Dogs are very space-oriented. Their kennel is their home." Lee built a heated, four-season kennel behind his house, and as his dogs mature, this becomes their year-round home. They've been assimilated to the kennel from puppyhood. "One of the reasons I decided to have [an outdoor] kennel was to train them to be space-oriented to the kennel." This helps immensely when you're traveling with the dog—you can be sure the dog will respond to the "kennel" command. This also works if you keep the dog in the house—sometimes, you will need to put it in the kennel for a timeout, a nice fallback during a dinner party.

I was curious about how old a puppy is when Lee starts training it. Roz broke in: "Well, Lee starts training from the day the dog comes home." Lee added, "I want the dogs to like what it is they're doing." Roz asked him to describe the hide-behind-the-tree method to get the dog to hunt close and come on command.

Lee lowered his voice: "Puppies are like children. If you took a five-year-old kid by the hand and were walking down on Thirty-fourth Street in New York at Christmastime, looking at all the nice things, and the kid let go of your hand, and there in a store window was this wonderful display of all these electric trains, but you decided to walk on and left the kid, when the kid turned around, he would panic: 'Where's daddy?' Same thing with a dog; same thing with a puppy.

"So I take my dogs into the woods, and I hide behind a tree. And I say nothing; I don't whistle. And all of a sudden, the puppy goes, 'Where is he?' What's the puppy gonna do? Soon as he comes back and gets anywhere near the tree, I step out, but I don't want to shock the puppy, so I lean out and say, 'Hey, good boy.'"

"And we give him cheese!" Roz added.

"Roz buys inexpensive cheese—I call it rat cheese, 'cause it's what you use in traps to catch rats—and I break a little piece off, and I reward him, so when he comes to me, he's rewarded. I'm accomplishing a lot of things here. The dog's found me, I'm his savior, and he gets rewarded! Then I start doing it with a one-blast whistle. When they get a little older, you can stop the treats; otherwise, you'll be spending a fortune on cheese.

"Now, if I were training a bird dog to hunt prairie grouse in South Dakota, Wyoming, Nebraska, eastern Montana, I would never do that. Then you want your dog to get out there. But in our New England grouse woods—and Minnesota, Michigan, Wisconsin—you want your dog to check back with you. If the dog is checking back with you, you don't need to communicate verbally or with the whistle.

"I train my puppies, when I take them in the woods, to walk the same trail each and every day. I know where they are; they know where I am." A field-trial dog is different, Lee says. "You want that dog to be bold; you want that dog to be a charger. You introduce those dogs to different spaces. But you take the dog on the same trail every day; you're teaching that dog, don't go too far. That's what you want when you hunt grouse and woodcock.

"There are several different means through which dogs learn. One of the most important is association through repetition. Repetition is the mother of all learning. Repeat things over and over and over again, until it's second nature to the dog. Another important thing is that you have to be in control—not only of the dog, but of yourself. When I first started to train, I used to lose my temper because I got frustrated. But eventually I learned that the best way to train a dog is to control a situation and not let the situation control you. If you're in control, it's much easier to train the dog. Period."

Putting the principles of training—particularly those I learned while observing professional trainers work—into practice during hunting seemed very complex to me. I asked Lee how he did this.

"Well," he said, "part of training is being a disciplinarian. Let's say you walk in on point and the bird goes out and you raise your gun and shoot. You miss and the bird keeps on flying, and the dog sees that the bird is going through the covert, and he breaks point before you give the command and starts chasing the bird. If you've trained this dog to be steady to wing and shot, you have *got* to let the dog know you're unhappy with that. That doesn't mean that you grab him by the scruff of the neck and beat him. What I do when a dog does that, I take my blaze orange cap off, put it over the barrels of the gun to prevent any debris from falling into the barrels, and lean the gun against a tree. I try to set it where there's a crotch and the gun can't fall. Then I go over to the dog and pick it up, literally take it up off of its fours, take it back to where it was, put it down, and say, 'Whoa; when you find the bird, whoa.' And it knows, 'cause we've done this before; we've done this with training pigeons."

Lee uses pigeons during training, with the help of his ever-patient wife. "She shoots the blank pistol, and I control." He plants the pigeons and works on steady to wing and shot in the same manner as I've described a professional trainer doing it earlier in this book.

Lee does not tolerate disobedience during steady-to-wing-and-shot training. "If you do things properly early in the dog's career," he said, "you will have a longer successful career of shooting birds over the dog. If you give the dog slack because you're interested only in killing the bird, you're gonna have a very sloppy dog. You will not have a class dog. Your dog will point, but as soon as the bird leaves the ground, that dog is after it. By the way, that's a good way to accidentally shoot your dog, too, particularly on woodcock, the males. Male woodcock go low. I cut my dogs no slack on any of that—but that doesn't mean I'm mean to them."

Lee has informed opinions about hunting with a pointing dog. We could call this "beyond the training" experience, or practical application of the training. We talked about this after hunting in Vermont's Northeast Kingdom one October afternoon. I shot one woodcock that flushed wild that day. We weren't so much interested in shooting birds that afternoon; we both wanted to watch Reilly and Lee's setters Harris and Holly work. We worked them one at a time, not together. It was early in the season, a rainy day, with tough conditions, and the thought of forcing the dogs to back and honor points (one dog not rushing in on another dog that's established point) seemed foolhardy and extreme.

"Something you've probably noticed," said Lee, "is that I try real hard not to use my voice when I'm hunting, and this goes back to Cliff Hale. First of all, although you may think you know more about bird hunting than the dog, the dog knows more about bird hunting than you do—the dog's programmed genetically for that. And I noticed that you say to Reilly, 'Come around.' You will see and have more shots at grouse the less you use your voice. You start using your voice in the woods, the birds are *whee-hoo*—gone. When I hunt with the dog by myself, I hardly ever use my voice; I rely on the whistle. Every now and then, I'll use my voice when I'm on a sidehill and the high pitch of the whistle doesn't work. But that's it."

Lee also told me that, though we all have the urge to yell at times, yelling at a dog is counterproductive. "Nagging at a dog is not good; it's like nagging at a kid: 'How much homework did you do? Did you finish your algebra? Blah, blah, blah.' After a while, the kid turns a deaf ear. Same thing with a dog. 'There he goes again, blowing that goddamn whistle. Blah, blah, blah.' Blow the whistle only when you really want the dog to turn or come around."

As I've mentioned, Lee does not work in the "real world" in the fall; he takes off four or five months to hunt birds. "All I do is shoot," he said. I asked this legend of the fall: "So when is the best shooting time?"

"The best time to hunt grouse, as a general rule in the Northeast, from Maine all the way to Minnesota, is the last two weeks in October and all of November. Okay, we have deer season in November in all of those states. But still, there are reasons for grouse hunting. The woodcock are gone, so you know the points are gonna be grouse. And the grouse hold better that time of year. Think of the plumage of a grouse—it's gray, brown, and black. No snow on the ground, the leaves are down, the vegetation is brown, and you get those cloudy days. Those grouse will rely on their camouflage; they'll just sit there, and the dog will go *bang:* 'There's your bird, boss.'

"Eight out of ten years, after deer season, there's snow on the ground. Two to four inches, the birds will be on the ground, scratching for beechnuts, scratching for apples; six inches or more, you should stay home with your dog. You might find somebody who'll disagree with that, but that's my opinion. I think that in grouse hunting, as in waterfowl hunting, bluebird days are your worst days. I like to hunt grouse on cloudy days. I like the sun to peek out every so often through the clouds, but I like it gray. An outdoor writer who wrote for the *Baltimore Sun,* Percy Blog, was an avid grouse hunter, and he said, 'There are no dull dark days.' Those are the best days to hunt; grouse lie better for a dog."

Chapter 17

Learning from a Pro, John Hayes at Kirby Mountain Kennels

In 2001, Reilly was with John Hayes at Kirby Mountain Kennels, and I intended to take advantage of his invitation to join him in his training whenever I could make the three-hour trip from southern Vermont. This was not the half-hour jaunt I had enjoyed several times each week the summer before when Reilly was with John Offerman. But John Hayes has a pied piper manner about him, and I knew I would be following him in the training field as often as I could.

John Hayes is exuberant, patient, a natural showman, an excellent teacher, and as excited about dog training today as he was when he started training dogs more than fifteen years ago. He has trained more than fifteen hundred dogs, about two-thirds pointers and the rest flushers, which means he has performed tens of thousands of training exercises. He has observed thousands of puppies and their early behaviors through his breeding program. He is fluent in the language of dog behavior.

To his clients, John recommends a gradualist training program for the first three years of a pointing dog's life: four to eight weeks the first year, six to twelve weeks the second and third. Following that, training and conditioning continue for the life of the dog. One of John's favorite aphorisms is from the great Oklahoma dogman Delmar Smith: "You are always training your dog, good and bad."

Reilly had about twelve weeks of training the previous summer, and then about eight months of pampering as a house dog by C and me. Let me say that I've never heard of a hunting dog and a house dog being mutually exclusive; a dog can be both, but you have to remember that your actions can and will affect the dog's performance, in the house and in the field. The first weekend I attended John's training sessions, after we shook hands and I asked how it was going, he said simply, "She's spoiled." He shrugged and laughed in his casual way of expressing the unstated. "I'm not gonna pull any punches here—face it, pal." Reilly had been with John for two weeks; it had taken him only about an hour or so, as he had told me it would, to know how C and I had treated her through the winter and spring.

I was chastened, of course, but not stung. Reilly needed discipline. John told me not to worry—he had seen the same example over and over. An owner feels guilty about leaving his dog at a kennel with a trainer—hell, the dog is part of the family!—and compensates when the dog returns home by slackening, if not abandoning, the rules of discipline. This is not to say, John told me, that you need to ride the dog hard or shock it with a collar into submission; that would be worse than being a pushover because it could injure the dog's ability to learn.

"Spoiling can be undone," he told me. "That's why you brought Reilly here. When I say spoiled, I don't mean only that you've given the dog tremendous care. You can walk the dog for three hours a day; you can make it beef stew—that's not spoiling the dog. Spoiling the dog is when you give it commands and you don't make it do the command. You know, many people talk to dogs and say, 'You wanna come over here?' I call that dog options. Well, there's no book about dog options—it's dog commands."

With a year's training under the dog's collar, so to speak, I expected John to tell me Reilly would fall right back into the pointer field-training program. Not so. When he brought her into the field the first few days she was with him, she was wild—straining against the check cord the whole time, not responding to commands, eager to hunt, though full of unfocused nervous energy.

"If I let her off this check cord, she'd be off to the next county," John said. I looked discouraged, and he saw this.

"Listen, in a family situation, your dog would be dead by now. Because a little kid would have opened the door and the dog would have run in the road and been killed. But with your lifestyle and your commitment to the dog, that did not happen. But you would not believe how often that happens for Brittanys and setters and pointers. A little kid opens the door, and the dog runs off and is killed. They've been bred for hundreds of years to run away; it's what they do."

And so began the process of retraining, before the next level of training could ensue—if, indeed, another level could ensue that summer. What would the next level be?

John's second-year pointer training works on staunchness on point, steady to wing when the bird flushes, steady to wing and shot, and retrieving to hand. If you plan to hunt your dog with others, he'll also include backing and honoring training for when more than one pointing dog is in the field hunting. One dog will point, and the second and third dogs will back up the point of the first. As they honor that dog's point, the backing dogs will not rush in to flush the pointed birds. It's a breathtaking sight: two or three or more trained pointers lined up and pointing a bird or a covey of birds. Multiple pointing dogs are often, if not always, run in quail fields down south so that lots of ground is covered, particularly when the hunters are on horseback—there they have a high vantage point from which to see distant points and can track quickly along with the dogs. It's quite common out west to run a brace or more of dogs as well—lots of room to run, lots of ground to cover. I haven't tried running Reilly with another dog yet, for fear that she'd get competitive and would bump birds. But I will one of these years. . . .

John Offerman had begun much of this second-year training with Reilly the previous summer, but I hadn't done any field work with her beyond conditioning—running her in the snowy fields around the house in winter and the woods in spring. I had maintained the all-important commands "whoa" and "come 'round," and I had done a modicum of style handling by stroking up Reilly's tail when she sight-pointed a robin or other songbird in the yard. John Hayes knew all this, of course—the dog's behavior told him the whole story.

Reilly needed a refresher of rudimentary field training—not so much a return to Class 101, but maybe a few weeks' revisiting. We'd take it slow, John said, working day by day. We'd have successes; we'd have slippages. But she'd get there, he assured me; she had good genes, and you can't change that. Repetition in the field and consistency with his handling, he said, were the keys. He would expose her to birds nearly every day, and this exposure would give her a hunting purpose, and the commands would begin to stick more and more.

Every Friday, I hastened from Bennington to get to I-91 and north to the Lyndonville area, where I checked into the modestly priced LynBurke Motel. The next day, I'd observe John with Reilly and other pointing dogs in training. Today still, John holds an open training session on Saturdays, and all clients are invited. Typically, that summer, five to seven dog owners showed up each weekend. We gathered by the dog trailer at eight or nine o'clock in the morning and then followed John dog by dog through the training field.

He'd release a dog from the dog-box trailer; introduce it to the audience and point out its owner, if the owner was there; have a helper plant several pigeons in bird ejectors, also called traps, in the field; and then run the dog through its paces as we followed along. John would instruct on what the dog was doing—ranging, hunting for itself, marking stale scent, getting birdy and going on point. He would whistle command the dog, without any verbal commands except "up" to get the dog working forward. When the dog established point, John would step back and address the crowd.

"Here's a three-year-old Brittany," he might say, "that we bred here at Kirby Mountain Kennels. She's had about forty weeks of training. Not bad, huh, Roger?"

Roger would laugh and smile.

"Like what you see?" John would prompt. The dog would still be on point, perhaps quivering its docked tail.

"Perfect, absolutely perfect," Roger would answer for the group.

John would nod to his helper, tell him to release the bird, and— *poof*—up would fling the pigeon from the radio-controlled trap. The dog, if exceptionally good, after all the waiting, might take a few steps as it marked the direction of the bird as John fired a starter's pistol several times, but it would not lunge toward the flushing bird.

Seeing this exercise a few times will leave you with no doubt about the value of professional pointing-dog training. The results can be remarkable: A ranging dog gets birdy; tightens its search to go on point, rigidly facing the planted bird; and holds that point for what seems like an eternity but is probably about one minute, as John speaks. You can walk in front of the dog, you can wave at it, you can trip a camera's shutter and pop a flash—the dog does not move. The bird is flushed by pressure from a hunter's boot or is sprung from a trap—whichever, the dog still holds point, perhaps swiveling its head to mark the flight path of the bird as John shoots from the starter's pistol.

Once the pigeon has flapped back toward John's barn, where the birds roost, John releases the dog. It buries its head into the scent circle and then proceeds forward as John whistles and says, "up." A thing of beauty.

John assured me that Reilly would do this—it would only take time. I agreed that she would stay for the entire summer at his kennel. I had travel planned in a few weeks, too, so it was better to have the dog in training than sitting in a boarding kennel or under the care of a dog sitter. I had lucked into meeting a master trainer and felt fully confident with Reilly being under John's watch.

When John ran Reilly on my next weekend at the farm, she was hunting much more under control. She established point but then began to creep. John "whoaed" her, picked her up under the belly and by the collar, and shook her two or three times. He placed her back on the spot where she originally went on point. He waited. He released the bird. He held her check cord as the bird flushed. She wiggled her tail, but didn't break clean free.

"Dogs hate to be off their feet," he said. "It immobilizes them, which, in the case of your dog, is a good thing. It's all part of the work. She has to know she can't get away with creeping or breaking."

John then turned to that morning's audience: "Joe knows that his dog was spoiled. But we're working that out." I admired John for his work. And, in the important roundabout of dog training, I was learning as much as the dog was, if not more. Reilly was fast improving toward the results that I wanted for her, and for me.

The next time I went to Kirby, in mid-August, I skipped the motel and instead camped at Island Pond in Brighton State Park. I arrived on Thursday in hard rain, and that weather continued on and off all weekend. Thursday night I was zipped tight in my tent out of the downpour, sipping beer and reading the real estate guides I had picked up at a rest area off I-91.

The weekend before, I had looked at some real estate in Newark, Vermont—camps, really, off the power grid and electrified by generator. Several were appealing, but I wanted more than a camp; I wanted a house with power and a phone line so I could work remotely at times. Buying up north was my plan. Sitting in my tent, I circled a few prospects in the guide—till I saw one listing for a small chalet-style house on Burke Mountain that was well within my price range.

I went to John's in the morning, watching him train Reilly and half a dozen other pointers. She was now holding steady to wing and shot and was staying steady as she marked birds after the flush. We wouldn't have time that summer, John said, to work on retrieving, but all signs were positive now on the field work.

Reilly had been with him for six weeks and was well into year-two training. Her pointing was staunch—body and head erect and tail high—and John was having the dog accomplish this, that weekend, without the use of an e-collar.

Later that day, I viewed the house—large yard, small unfinished outdoor building, good-size pond near the front of the property that was creek-fed from tributaries off Burke Mountain. The mountain was home of Burke Mountain Academy, the country's first ski academy, and an uncrowded ski area that I had never heard of before that summer. From the front door of that small house to the mid-Burke lift area was a ten-minute drive—to snowboarding.

I saw a couple other properties in the area, which I quickly abandoned to see the chalet house again. I liked the real estate agent, Annette. I liked the vibe emitting from the small mountain cottage, though it was a starter-slash-fixer-upper, to be sure. But the location on the side of a ski mountain, within walking distance of what appeared to be solid grouse coverts—areas ripe for spontaneous hunting such as my father enjoyed when he was young—was all that I wanted.

On Sunday, I stopped by Annette's office and made an offer.

Then I left for three weeks out west. I started with an overnight in Steamboat Springs and continued on to an Orvis fly-fishing media event in Kremmling, Colorado, at the cushy Elktrout Lodge. Afterward, Phil Monahan and I drove through Rocky Mountain National

Park to southern Wyoming, stayed a night in Laramie, and then headed north to Jackson to meet up with our friend Ed Scheff and fish with him for a few days before continuing on to Salt Lake City for the annual fly-fishing industry trade show.

One morning in Jackson, I was told over the phone by Annette that my offer on the cottage in East Burke, Vermont, was rejected. A couple hours later, I was told that my counteroffer was accepted. I was a homeowner.

I returned from Salt Lake late on September 9. My parents and my sister, Jennifer, who had been at a wedding that weekend in upstate New York, were waiting for me at my house in North Bennington. We partied a bit but called it a night early since I had to be at the fly-fishing magazine offices the next day. We had dinner together on September 10 and stayed up reminiscing to take advantage of our time together because, with Jenni living in California, these sorts of family gatherings happened only on Christmas or the Fourth of July, and this September get-together was a treat.

I was late for the office the morning of September 11. My hair was still wet as I kissed my mother good-bye and grabbed my briefcase and headed for the door. I was pausing to finish the bottom of my coffee cup when my father shouted from the living room, "Joe, you better get in here!"

It was about ten minutes to nine.

My father was watching one of the morning talk shows. On the TV screen, the top of one of the World Trade towers was smoldering. I have a mental picture now of gray smoke stretching in a line against a sunny blue background.

I thought of the times I had been in Windows on the World. I thought of the 1992 attack on the towers that happened when I lived in New York City. We were sent home from work that day. But my coworkers and I never felt any impending sense of danger.

I had been below 34th Street in 1992. Thank God, we all said, that the carnage was limited to fewer than ten people. God help those in the parking garage in 1992, we said.

How could that happen in America, in New York, we asked, sitting together in 1992, watching cable TV news, and wondering how quickly the towers would be fixed. There was never any question about the towers being fixed, repaired, reopened. Within days or weeks, not months. We didn't know any better at the time.

Now, sitting in my living room with my dad on September 11, 2001, my mother and sister in the kitchen still having a talk over coffee, I thought, "Damn, that hole's gonna be really hard to fix. That'll close the tower for a long time—probably months."

The announcer mentioned terrorism, but there was still speculation that a small plane had hit the tower. About that time, you could hear the deceleration of jet engines—I can still hear the sound, though I can't and won't try to render it in words—after which I saw the tail section of a plane and a plume of flame belch from the face of the other tower. The day now known as 9/11 was upon us. Incredibly, my family was with me. All but my brother, Tim, safe in Cleveland. And Reilly was in northern Vermont. I will always have a churn in the pit of my stomach when I think of that day. I am still moved close to weeping when I look down Fifth Avenue today.

My sister's flight from Albany to California had been scheduled for the afternoon of September 11. It was postponed for the foreseeable future, with the air-flight ban after the terrorist attack and to gird against the ensuing uncertainty and anthrax madness. My family stayed together for the next few days.

As a diversion, I suggested we head north to Lyndonville and Kirby, where I could get Reilly from John Hayes's kennel and we could have a peek at my soon-to-be house. We all checked into the LynBurke that night and talked about happy family memories and found solace in one another.

The next day, my mom and dad and sister and I went to John's to pick up Reilly, her twelve weeks of training complete.

"You have a beautiful family," John told me as he shook my hand; I said the same to him about his wife and kids and dogs in the house and yard. I handed him a check, and he handed me a report card—actually called an Evaluation and Progress Chart—for Reilly. It read, under classifications:

Temperament:	Very good
Biddability:	Very good
Desire:	Excellent
Birdiness:	Excellent
Pointing Instinct:	Very good
Nose:	Good-very good
Range:	Medium

There was also a progress report, which mirrored the ratings above, except for the "come" command, about which John had notated, "Very good (with e-collar)." So runaway issues were evident. Still, I read with pride John's handwritten comments on the back of the report: "The words that come to mind for Reilly are CLASS ACT. She has excelled beautifully this summer. Hunt this wonderful dog as much as possible; that is all she needs at this time. Be firm but fair with her, and enjoy the journey as much as the destination. Good luck & great hunting, John."

This came after sixty-seven days of training and observation. John had taken to calling Reilly a "rock star" in the later weeks of training, as she hunted with reckless-though-gaining-control abandon in the training field. So I adapted my thinking of Reilly's hunting manner to "rock-star style."

John's evaluative comments, to me, once more proved that having a dog trainer isn't an instant fix to your dog's problems, but it sure is an aid to figuring out the process.

We left John's kennels, Reilly, my sister, and I, and drove up Burke Mountain on the scenic road to the summit, where I let the dog run for a while down and across the ski trails till she was run out and calmed for our ride back to North Bennington. My folks left to return to their house in central New York, anxious for the ferry ride across Lake Champlain and the comforting views of the Adirondack Mountains. The Vermont bird season would be opening in fewer than twenty days. Reilly and I would put her rock-star status to the test. I reveled in having my dog back with me, such a comfort in light of the circumstances at that time. Jenni and I headed south. We didn't say much. We didn't need to. My sister and I have always had a telepathy that redeems us from speaking yet still has us patched into one another's emotions if not thoughts. That was a tough time in life, the week of September 11, 2001. Getting Reilly back helped. Having my sister close helped more.

Jenni got on her flight for California that weekend. The next day, I started getting Reilly ready for bird-hunting season, working with her on the lawn to drive home the operative commands of "whoa" and "come 'round" and "heel." I put up a for-sale sign on the travel trailer—I would be closing on my mountain cottage in early October and didn't need another Grouse House—and sat down inside with *Wing & Shot* to review again the teachings of Robert Wehle and how they applied to my dog. In my left ear—the one in which dreams are always amplified—I heard John Hayes address us bird-dog owners: "You are always training your dog, good and bad."

So far, Reilly had done well. So far, I had learned enough to know that I would do well, too, working with her. Sitting inside my trailer. The dog sprawled on the bed. I rubbed Reilly's back, and she groaned in pleasure, telling me, "Dad, I've been away at camp for the past couple of summers, and I'm glad I'm home, but I learned a lot, and it'll all work out fine."

So were the words of my dog, reported by me.

Afterword

I WISH I COULD SAY THAT WHEN REILLY CAME HOME FROM HER SECOND year of hunting-dog training, she maintained the rock-star pointer status she attained at Kirby Mountain Kennels and applied this to the hunting woods. No, that didn't happen. John Hayes worked with Reilly on (quoting from his literature) "staunch on point . . . handling in cover . . . whoa and yard work . . . no chasing allowed," and she did an exemplary job in his training fields. But after Reilly returned home from twelve weeks in the kennel, back in the real world, she continued her runaway ways when I took her out into the grouse woods.

One episode saw my friend Phil Monahan hunting with Reilly and me in southern Vermont. The dog didn't point or flush a single bird in about an hour's hunting session, as she ranged out farther and farther from my commands. When two kids riding fat-tired all-terrain vehicles passed us on a two-track logging road, Reilly broke for it and followed them off into nowhere. Well after dark, after I'd spent an hour calling and whistling for her, the kids came down the logging road to Phil and me and asked, "Is that your dog up the trail there?"

Of course it was Reilly. The hunt was long over. Perhaps she'd been frustrated by not finding birds and decided to follow a more interesting path than hunting by running with the ATVs. I called her along and we went back to my truck. I didn't use the e-collar; we simply walked in silence with her on the check cord, till I kenneled her in the back of my truck and we headed for home.

Phil and I had a beer or two in my kitchen, and I apologized for the failed hunt. Reilly curled up near Phil's feet. Phil rubbed her head, telling her, "Uncle Phil's not mad; he's yer buddy."

A couple weeks later, on Columbus Day weekend, Phil and I went north to Lyndonville and stayed at the LynBurke Motel, where we tried to wait out the rain. When the autumn downpours tapered off enough to make for a reasonable hunting atmosphere in the woods, we didn't find many birds. I released Reilly in a field to tire her out some, and she promptly ran off. I called and she wouldn't come. It was as if she knew what I knew: Her e-collar was out of juice, so no punishment was forthcoming. With the rain pattering on the leaves and her bell ringing in her ears, she probably couldn't hear me yelling. And then I heard the bell, and then here was a soggy white dog bounding toward me. Not wanting to punish a dog for coming to hand, I told her "Good girl" till she was snug in the kennel in the wayback of my truck, and we went back to the motel.

Both episodes proved to be apt reminders that a professional pointing-dog trainer is not a panacea for all that behaviorally ails a young hunting dog. "Work in progress" is the phrase that seems most appropriate for a two-year-old pointer. Reilly would develop in her own time—and clearly she needed more time for that.

That season, I continued to hold back from shooting wild-flushing birds. I worked Reilly in the woods with the check cord, having her drag it in light coverts, and setting her loose in heavy brush so that she could learn for herself the specific areas in which she might find birds—grouse near apple trees and wild cranberry vines, woodcock in soggy-bottomed lowlands grown up with slashy trees. Her progression was good—she was learning her way around coverts; she was showing maturity.

Still, frustrations continued. I spent one hunting afternoon with Lee Leone in his coverts outside of Island Pond in northern Vermont. We hunted Lee's seasoned English setter and found nothing. When it was Reilly's turn, she busted a covey of grouse, about eight birds—not a common occurrence to flush so many grouse in northern Vermont at once. Lee was disappointed that after about an hour of hunting through some snagging coverts, it didn't go our way. Reilly did not point one bird; she just flew headlong into chasing bird after bird, disregarding my calls and whistles and even, finally, my taps on the e-collar activator. When the embarrassment of flushes was over, Lee said to me wearily, "You need a better collar on her."

Reilly's fit of avian pursuit was everything John Hayes had worked to diminish that summer. I swallowed my anger and frustration. What could be done now? What would punishment accomplish except to make me feel better?

The dog was wearing an inexpensive, limited-range collar I had bought the year before when I considered her a puppy, when I was hesitant to use an e-collar at all. John Hayes trained Reilly with an e-collar; he had stressed to me that it was humane if used correctly, and it certainly was the best tool with which to shape a pointer for hunting work, when obedience and biddability are all-important.

Standing in the woods with Lee, Reilly still ranging out of view, though within bell range, I was embarrassed. Lee knows dogs. He knows when a dog screws up. He knows it's not so much the dog that screws up but the owner, often by taking the wrong action to discipline the dog, either overpunishing it and possibly compromising the dog's instinct to hunt, or by taking no action at all and thereby reinforcing the dog's inappropriate behavior. I asked him what I could do now. Learning from a trainer in July or August is one thing, under desirable conditions when the birds are readily planted and won't run from the dog—but what do you do when you're on your own in the hunting woods?

"Just get a better electronic collar," he told me. "And use it to let her know that you're not going to let her hunt by herself."

I had heard the same advice from Tim Leary after we hunted one afternoon in one of his apple orchard coverts. Reilly bounded away from us, a white streak in the brown woods, and before Tim could get to her at the edge of some pines, we both heard the thrumming flushes of two grouse. Reilly heard them, too, and was off like a cannonball to find them. After calling and whistling to get her back, I put her on the check cord, apologizing, and we headed back to the truck. Tim complimented the dog, said the rainy conditions made it hard for her to sniff out bird scent—and then told me that I should consider an e-collar with greater range. "You gotta let her know as soon as she breaks that you're not gonna stand for that," Tim told me as we shared apple slices and sharp Cabot cheddar off the tailgate of my truck.

I got a new collar, though I held out till the next season to spend the $360 or so that it cost. I got the collar for Reilly that John Hayes trains with—in fact, I asked John to order it for me. The Dogtra 2000 model has a signal of more than a mile, so it was quite helpful as a tool with which to train Reilly to stay within a hunting range of twenty yards or so. At that distance, I can clearly hear her bell or the collar's beeper sounding, and in thin woods, I can see her and easily catch up to her when she's on point. The upgrade to a "pro" (as the maker calls it) e-collar has made a clear difference in years three and beyond, hunting with Reilly.

Also during the 2001 season, Brendan Banahan came to my recently purchased house in the Northeast Kingdom to hunt with Reilly and his pointer, Nell, who at thirteen was still game to hunt, though now laboring.

We didn't dare hunt Reilly and Nell together—Nell was in no mood to play with puppies—so we gave each dog a turn in a good woodcock covert bordering a river. Reilly worked fine and hunted close in this thick stuff, but she found no birds. Out came the experienced dog, into the sunny woods of northern Vermont on an October afternoon. She pointed two woodcock; I shot them both. They were the last birds Nell pointed; cancer did its dirty work that winter.

I took Reilly to John Hayes's in late summer 2002 for a month-long third-year curriculum. John told me when I visited that she had figured out the training-field pointing game. The smart dogs do that after a while, he said; they anticipate where the pigeons will be planted, the one downside of repetition. To solve that particular bit of canine cunning, and "to really put the heat on a dog," he says, John introduces confusion drills. Here, he plants four or more pigeons in launchers arranged in an arc or a circle. When the dog points one, he'll eject a bird behind the dog or to the side of it.

The goals are to keep the dog absolutely steady to wing and shot and to have it naturally begin to sight-mark the flushed birds, if it shows an interest in doing so. The confusion—really, multiple distractions for the dog—helps the dog assimilate to real-world hunting situations, in which several birds may flush yet the dog still must stay in control and not break wildly after the errant-flushing birds.

Reilly passed the drills with flying colors. It was time again to get her into the woods. At three years old, she was an ace on woodcock, holding point on a bird forever and a day—a good response from a young pointer. Grouse here in northern Vermont, where they have developed an acute running gene, were more difficult. She pointed a handful of birds, six total, and I shot one that season. After shooting six woodcock, and having friends shoot a few others, over her, I closed the hunting on those less-than-abundant migratory birds.

After three summers of professional pointer training for Reilly, I have shot fewer than forty birds over her; friends have shot three or four others. In those three years, I averaged a total of about twenty hours of hunting each season. I didn't care a whit about bag numbers; one bird, or even none at all, would be just fine. Just watching Reilly grow into her skills was all I wanted.

One of the best commentaries about working with a professional trainer is that of Tim Leary, an opinionated dog owner who for decades trained his own dogs. He began in 2002 to take his two young setters over to Kirby Mountain Kennels for an almost daily training regimen. Tim had worked a setter with John in the past, but not on such a strict schedule. That year, Tim told me how he had gained an appreciation for the work that a professional trainer could do; after all those years training his own dogs, grinding it out, he was seeing the immediate results of John Hayes working with his setters. Tragically, Tim never got to hunt with the dogs at their mature best; he died in a construction accident in 2003.

John Hayes has some advice for dog owners contemplating professional training. Most important, he says, is to visit the kennel first without your dog. Get a feel for the environment and watch the trainer work with dogs; if your dog is not present, you can make a dispassionate judgment.

Once the training begins, tune in. "If you don't understand why the trainer is doing what he's doing, ask questions. He uses discipline not to be a hard guy, but to get results. This is not puppy kindergarten, so give the trainer freedom to work."

Be realistic about how long training may take, even if you have a bundle of genetic joy. "I joke about reading in this or that magazine about the six-month-old dog who just went to Nebraska or Kansas and hunted six species of birds and did all this. Well, the dog may have been in the car, and it may have run around in a field, and maybe pointed a bird or picked up a bird. But did it really do all that stuff? I don't believe it." John has owned more than seventy hunting dogs, and he's never had a pointing dog perform at a seasoned level at six months. His Brittany will point between seventy and seventy-five grouse in a season, "but this dog has had twelve months' training and tons of experience, and he's five years old."

When is it time to take the dog home? "You want the dog home four to eight weeks before hunting season. The owner needs to grow into what the dog has learned, and the dog needs to learn to obey you. Remember, you dropped off a dog that didn't listen to you, and guess what? Unless you change your behavior, it's still not gonna listen to you! I didn't give the dog chances not to listen to me. I used an electronic collar. I didn't abuse the dog, but I gave the dog chances to succeed, and anytime it didn't I was there to correct it. Here's a quote to live by: Hope your dog always does great things, but always be prepared for failure. Every time I take a dog out, I'm hoping it shines. But I am not disappointed or upset or even surprised when the dog fails, because . . . they all do. Whenever a dog fails, go back to where it was successful, and quit on a high note."

Working with professional trainers has changed my bird hunting forever. A good dog will probably figure out its role in the woods eventually, but I felt a responsibility to get Reilly to her natural level of performance as best I could. She was a hunting dog, a pointer, from champion bloodlines, and I wanted her to have the best possible training to help bring out her natural abilities. I wanted her to develop those abilities without any mishandling from a first-time pointer owner.

I could not be happier with the results, and the fact that I have years ahead of me to hunt with this dog as well as about three hundred days each year outside of hunting season on which to enjoy her company. Just Reilly and me, doing whatever it is we do, around the house and the yard. But I work constantly to reinforce the hunting training she's had.

Taking your pointing dog to a professional trainer requires a commitment on your part—not only financially, but also to accept the obligation to learn what the trainer is doing. Knowing the process and the work involved will allow you to carry on the principles of good training while you hunt and—perhaps more important for the overall behavior of your dog—all year long. These are principles you can carry over a lifetime of bird hunting with a lifetime of pointing dogs. A professional trainer will not only help your dog achieve its highest potential, he'll make you a better dog owner—if you're willing to listen and learn.

BIBLIOGRAPHY

De La Valdene, Guy. *Making Game: An Essay on Woodcock.* Oshkosh,
WI: Willow Creek Press, 1985.

The Monks of New Skete. *The Art of Raising a Puppy.* New York,
Boston, London: Little, Brown and Company, 1991.

Roebuck, Kenneth C. *Gun-Dog Training Pointing Dogs.* Mechanicsburg, PA: Stackpole Books, 1983.

Wehle, Robert G. *Snakefoot: The Making of a Champion.* Henderson,
NY: Country Press, 1996.

———. *Wing & Shot.* Henderson, NY: Country Press, 1979.